THE
WHOLE
BIBLE STORY

THE
WHOLE
BIBLE STORY

Everything That Happens in the Bible

DR. WILLIAM H. MARTY

BETHANYHOUSE

a division of Baker Publishing Group
Minneapolis, Minnesota

Published by Bethany House Publishers
11400 Hampshire Avenue South
Bloomington, Minnesota 55438
www.bethanyhouse.com

Bethany House Publishers is a division of
Baker Publishing Group, Grand Rapids, Michigan

Printed in the United States of America

Library of Congress Cataloging-in-Publication Data
Names: Marty, William Henry, author.
Title: The whole Bible story : everything that happens in the Bible / William
    H. Marty.
Description: Minneapolis, Minnesota : Bethany House, a division of Baker
    Publishing Group, [2021] | Audience: Ages: 8-12
Identifiers: LCCN 2021028780 | ISBN 9780764238871 (paperback) | ISBN
    9780764239670 | ISBN 9781493433704 (ebook)
Subjects: LCSH: Bible stories, English.
Classification: LCC BS551.3 .M37 2021 | DDC 220.95/05—dc23
LC record available at https://lccn.loc.gov/2021028780

Cover design by Dan Pitts
Cover and interior illustrations by Heath McPherson

Baker Publishing Group publications use paper produced from sustainable
forestry practices and post-consumer waste whenever possible.

21   22   23   24   25   26   27   7   6   5   4   3   2   1

Contents

1

From Creation to Babel

GENESIS 1-11

WHO'S WHO

» **God (the Lord)**—God creates the world and then his people go and mess it all up

» **Adam and Eve**—the first couple ever created; they run around naked

» **Satan**—he shows up and ruins all the fun

» **Cain and Abel**—two brothers who brought new meaning to "sibling rivalry"

» **Noah**—the guy who made the first cruise ship . . . for animals

WHERE ARE WE?

» **Garden of Eden**—paradise and all-you-can-eat fruit trees (except for one)

» **Mesopotamia**—some country that's hard to spell

INTERESTING STUFF IN THIS SECTION

» The first wedding. No rice was thrown.

» The first murder. God was the only eyewitness.

» The oldest man in the Bible. Methuselah, 969 years old. That's a lot of candles on one cake.

» The first ship is built. It was like three football fields long. Pretty good for a first-time shipbuilder.

» The first rainbow in the sky.

» Our calendar week is based on the seven days of creation.

It All Begins (GENESIS 1–2)

In the beginning, God created everything out of nothing. His Spirit hovered over the creation, looking over every detail in this huge project.

God built everything through a simple word. He said "light," and light appeared. He said "sky," and sky appeared. He did the same for the land, the seas, the plants and trees, the sun, the moon, and the stars, then all the birds, sea creatures, and animals. He liked everything he made and called it good.

Then God said, "Let's make people in our image and let them rule over everything we created." So God made male and female and told them to be fruitful and multiply themselves throughout the earth. He liked them a whole lot, calling them "very good."

God rested after all those six days of creation, calling the seventh day a day of rest, so people could take a break to remember God and all he had done.

Let's go back to day six and see specifically how the creation of people happened. God made a beautiful garden in a place called Eden. It had all the fruit trees you could ever imagine. God took some dirt, blew life into it, and made a man. God told the man to eat whatever he wanted in that garden, but God made one rule: "Do not eat from a tree called the Knowledge of Good and Evil or you will die."

> We are not God, but we are like him in qualities such as love, intelligence, reason, compassion, etc.

Then God looked at the man who was all by himself and for the first time said something was "not good." God said, "I should make a suitable helper for him." First, he asked the man to go and name all the animals. As he did, the man realized every animal had a partner, male and female, and little baby animals. The man realized he was missing something.

God then put the man to sleep and performed surgery on him, removing a piece of his side, and created a woman out of it. The man, Adam, called her Eve and said, "This woman is my bone and my flesh." God brought them together, uniting them, like a wedding. In the future, a man and woman will leave their parents and start a new family and become one.

It All Falls Apart (GENESIS 3–5)

Satan showed up, disguised as a snake, and convinced the woman to eat from that Knowledge of Good and Evil tree. Satan tempted Eve by calling God a liar, making her doubt what God said and whether they really would die if they ate the fruit. Eve bought into what Satan said and disobeyed God, tasting the delicious fruit for herself, then giving Adam a bite.

Satan's name is not mentioned here, but later in the Bible—in Ezekiel and Revelation—he's identified as the ancient serpent who invaded the garden.

Guilt washed over them. They realized, "Uh-oh, we messed up." They had been running around naked, but now they felt ashamed and needed to cover themselves up. Adam and Eve found fig leaves and sewed them together, and they covered up their private areas.

God showed up, wanting to see his favorite creations, and wondered where everyone was. Adam and Eve hid, afraid and embarrassed because they disobeyed God. They blamed each other and that devious ol' snake, Satan. God had to punish them for disobedience, making life hard and painful, eventually leading to death. They were kicked out of Paradise and told life would be hard for them.

Adam and Eve had a couple sons—Cain, who worked with livestock, and Abel, who planted crops. Cain was jealous of Abel's offering to God, so Cain killed Abel. God saw what Cain did and made him leave. So Cain left his family and started a new home in a place called Nod. Adam and Eve later had another son named Seth, which made them very happy.

During a long period of time after this, people started having more kids, more families. People lived a long time, like Adam to 930 years old. But a guy named Methuselah lived even longer—969 years. Though people lived longer than we do today, as a consequence of sin, everyone eventually died. The world population grew and expanded, but as it did, people were getting meaner and more wicked.

Ark-eology (GENESIS 6–9)

Noah was a good man. God loved him because Noah walked faithfully with God. But Noah was the last good person on earth. Things were that bad.

There were women from a godly line of people having babies with an ungodly line of big, physical giants, like pro wrestlers (The Rock). They were all about power and getting their way. God saw the trend and needed to stop it.

God told Noah he was going to punish the whole earth with a flood and wipe out everyone, for a complete and total population reboot. He asked Noah to build a huge ship (ark) to hold his family and two of every kind of species of animal. After God gave Noah the dimensions for the building project, Noah went to work. It was three stories high and as long as three football fields. Once it was completed, God started leading animals to the ark. Noah, his wife, and their three sons—Shem, Ham, and Japheth—and their wives all got on board. Eight people were on the ark, plus a bunch of animals.

Then a horrible rain fell from the sky and water burst out of the ground. Immediately it flooded the earth, drowning every person and animal not on the ark. Only Noah's family and those animals survived. It rained, in total, for forty days and forty nights. Noah and his family

had to wait to get off the ark until the water evaporated, exposing the land.

God made a promise to Noah, saying he'd never cause another flood to destroy the world. He put a rainbow in the sky as a reminder of that promise.

Nations and Towers (GENESIS 10-11)

Lots of time passed as more and more people were born. From them, nations grew and great cities populated. Everyone in all these cities began to talk with each other, and many of them came up with an idea. They decided to build a huge tower to reach the heavens so they could make themselves famous. They wanted this city to bring everyone together and stay in one place instead of going out to fill the earth, like God commanded.

God saw this and became very concerned. They were becoming mean like the people before the flood. God

13

sighed and thought, *Since they all speak the same language, they are discussing these terrible ideas.* So God confused their languages, stopping their evil plans. Since they couldn't understand each other, they split up and moved all over the world. The languages of the world started at that time.

One family came from Noah's son Shem. They lived in an area called Mesopotamia, also known as Ur. A man named Terah had a son named Abram. Abram married a beautiful woman named Sarai, but sadly they couldn't have any children. God was about to fix all that.

WHAT'S THE POINT?

▶ God designed the world so his favorite creation would have a wonderful place to live. Sadly, people disobeyed God over and over and over.

▶ God must punish sin. He can't just look the other way. Jesus will come to earth to right the wrong that Satan caused.

▶ God is very patient and always helping people get closer to himself.

▶ People naturally want to sin; God has to step in and stop us from destroying ourselves.

2

The Abrahams

GENESIS 12–50

 WHO'S WHO

» **Abraham**—his name was Abram but God changed it to Abraham, meaning "father of all nations."

» **Sarah**—her name was Sarai but God changed it to Sarah, meaning "mother of all nations."

» **Lot**—Abraham's nephew and a little troublemaker

» **Ishmael**—a son born to Abram (before he was Abraham) through a surrogate woman named Hagar

» **Isaac**—Abraham and Sarah's son born when they were in their eighties and nineties!

» **Esau**—the son of Isaac and Rebekah, a twin, whose name means "hairy"

» **Jacob**—the son of Isaac and Rebekah, a twin, who technically came out second but worked really hard to become the firstborn son

» **Joseph**—Jacob's favorite son who became the vice president of Egypt

17

WHERE ARE WE?

» **Mesopotamia**—known as Ur and Haran

» **Land of Canaan**—known later as Israel and the Promised Land

» **Egypt**—you know, the place of pyramids

INTERESTING STUFF IN THIS SECTION

» Ur is only one of two biblical places that have two letters in their names. The other is Ai.

» Isaac's name means "laughter."

» The twelve sons born to Isaac will later be known as the twelve tribes of Israel.

» Judah is called a lion. Jesus came from the line of Judah. Aslan, from *The Lion, the Witch and the Wardrobe*, represents Jesus, that lion.

Honest Abe (GENESIS 12–18)

God called out to Abram and said, "Pack up your family and go to the place that I'm going to show you." Then God told him something that changed the entire course of history. He said, "I'm going to make a great nation out of you, and I will bless you. I will make your name great and you will bless others. I will bless those who bless you and curse those who curse you. Everyone ever born will be blessed through you." Wow.

Abram heard this and moved, without any other instructions, from a place called Ur to Canaan, which we know as Israel today. Abram did well there, his flocks growing. God told him he would give all this land to Abram's children. Abram wondered, *Children? Okay . . . but I'm in my nineties.*

Many believe that Jesus would be the blessing that would come to all nations, as spoken by God to Abram.

A famine hit the land, so Abram, Sarai, and Lot went to Egypt. The leader of Egypt, Pharaoh, saw how beautiful Sarai was and wanted her for himself. Abram, afraid the Egyptians would kill him to take her away, lied and said, "She's my sister." When Pharaoh took her, a plague hit his household. Pharaoh realized Abram's lie was behind the plague and he kicked them out.

Abram became very wealthy (remember God said he would bless him). Lot's herds and tents grew also, and the land couldn't support two businesses. So Lot decided to take the land east of the Jordan River (called Jordan today), and Abram took the land west of it (Israel today).

A bunch of kings in the area decided to fight, and two cities, Sodom and Gomorrah, were attacked. Lot, and everything he had, was taken captive. Abram put together a small army of 318 men to rescue Lot. They became heroes.

A king of Salem (a city known later as Jerusalem) named Melchizedek came out and blessed Abram. He was also a

Melchizedek also brought wine and bread to Abram, similar to the wine and bread Jesus used at his Last Supper.

priest, so Abram gave him an offering (or tithe) of 10 percent of his possessions.

Again, God showed up to remind Abram about his promise to create a great nation from all the children Abram will have. Abram said, "But I'm in my nineties and still have no children." God told him to go outside and look at all the stars in the sky. "That's how many offspring you will have."

Abram looked at the sky and saw all the stars. He believed and trusted God. At that moment, Abram was right with God.

But Abram was not perfect, and Sarai, fed up with waiting so long to be a mom, told Abram to use a servant girl named Hagar as a substitute to have his baby, but then give it to Sarai. Abram did as Sarai asked, but Sarai mistreated Hagar (she was obviously jealous), and Hagar ran

away. God found her and comforted her, telling her to go back home. God predicted this child, named Ishmael, would be a wild, hostile man to everyone.

Abram, now ninety-nine years old, heard from God again. God changed his name to Abraham, meaning "father of all nations." He renamed Sarai *Sarah*, calling her the "mother of all nations." This was a strange title since she was in her eighties and still had not had a child. So she laughed at the whole idea.

God said, "Since you laughed, you'll call him Isaac, which means 'laughter.'"

Partly Cloudy with a Chance of Brimstone
(GENESIS 19–20)

Later, three heavenly visitors showed up to Abraham's tents. Abraham told Sarah to make them something to eat. While they talked, one of the angels mentioned stopping by in a year to see Abraham's son (which wasn't even in a womb yet). Off to the side, Sarah laughed . . . again. She tried to deny that she laughed, but she laughed.

The three men looked down on Sodom and Gomorrah, saying that the Lord has heard the cry from these cities, and it's time to wipe them out. Abraham pleaded with God to spare the cities, wondering if fifty righteous people was enough to stop the destruction. God knew there weren't fifty good people there. Abraham tried another number—forty-five—then forty, thirty-five, thirty, all the way to ten. God said, "If you can find ten good people, I won't destroy it."

Two of the angels went into Sodom. The people of the town treated them poorly, threatening and mocking them. They went to Lot's house and got him, his wife, and two daughters out. Then came a hailstorm of fire from the sky, destroying the city and wiping out all the people. One of the angels had told Lot and his family not to look back, but Lot's wife did, and she immediately turned to a pillar of salt. She should have listened.

Lot and his daughters survived, hiding in a cave.

Abraham moved his wife, Sarah, to an area named Gerar and did that whole "she's my sister" thing because she was so beautiful (now in her nineties!). The king took Sarah but God spoke to him in a dream and said, "Don't touch her!" He returned Sarah and gave Abraham a bunch of cattle and sheep, plus bags of silver. It all turned out well for Abraham.

The One-Hundred-Year-Old Dad (GENESIS 21-23)

Finally, Sarah became pregnant and gave birth to a son whom they named Isaac. Abraham was one hundred years old. Now Sarah really laughed, this time with joy.

Sarah saw Hagar and Ishmael mocking Isaac and wanted them sent away. Abraham was displeased with the order—Ishmael was Abraham's own son, after all. But God promised to take care of them. Abraham led them away while God promised to make Ishmael a mighty nation.

Then came a big test. God came to Abraham and told him to sacrifice his son as a burnt offering on a mountain in Moriah. Abraham trusted God and obediently did what he asked. He arrived at the mountain and climbed it with his son, who carried the wood and rope.

Isaac looked around and wondered, "Where's the burnt offering?" Abraham responded, "God will provide."

Abraham placed Isaac on the wood, bound and tied, and lifted the knife—trusting God all the way—until an angel stopped him, saying, "You passed the test. You fear God and did not withhold your son." God, at that moment, provided a ram, whose horns were caught in the thicket. That ram was a substitute for Isaac and died instead.

Sarah lived thirty-some years more, then died. Abraham bought property from the Hittites and buried her in a cave

> Two thousand years later, God would provide his own son on the same mountain, dying for all our sins. Not a ram, but the Lamb of God.

called Machpelah. Abraham married another woman named Keturah and he had lots of sons through her.

The Rise of Isaac (GENESIS 24–25:18)

Isaac was a full-grown man and ready to marry, but Abraham wanted him to get a wife from his ancestors. Abraham ordered a servant to go back to the land they came from—Mesopotamia—and find a wife for his son. The servant arrived at a well and prayed, "Lord, help me find a wife for my master's son."

As he prayed, a woman walked up to the well, and she was really beautiful. Her name was Rebekah. The servant told her the story and she was amazed. Rebekah took the servant back to her family and told them the story. They were blown away, including Rebekah's brother, Laban. This had to be God working.

The servant came back to Isaac with Rebekah and it was love at first sight. They got married when he was forty years old, and they were totally in love.

Soon after, Abraham, happy to see his son married, died and left everything to Isaac. Abraham was 175 years old. Isaac and Ishmael buried him at Machpelah, where Sarah was previously laid to rest. Ishmael lived a little bit longer, to 137 years old. His descendants moved down toward Egypt.

Jacob the Trickster (GENESIS 25:19-27:46)

Twenty years after their wedding, Rebekah was not able to have a child until Isaac prayed for her. She got pregnant with twins. The babies wrestled around inside her womb. Rebekah wondered what was going on. God told her there were two nations inside her, one would be stronger than the other, and the older one would serve the younger—which was strange, because the youngest always served the older.

The two babies competed even at their birth. The first one came out red and hairy. They called him Esau (which means "hairy"). As he came out, the second one clung to his heel, trying to cross the finish line at the same time. They named him Jacob, which means "heel-grabber."

Esau grew up loving to hunt. Isaac liked him. Jacob was a mama's boy, hanging out in the kitchen, so Rebekah liked him more.

One day, Jacob made a stew, and Esau came in from a long hunting trip, hungry and ready to eat. He smelled the stew and said, "Give me some of that!"

Jacob, still wanting to be the firstborn son, said, "Sell me your birthright. I want to be first."

Esau threw up his hands. "Fine, take it. What good will being firstborn be if I die of hunger." Esau gave Jacob the position and ate his lentil stew.

Another famine hit the area, just like it did with Abraham. God told Isaac to go to Gerar, where Abimelek, the king of the Philistines, ruled. When the men of the town saw Rebekah's beauty, they inquired about her. Isaac pulled a trick out of Abraham's bag and said, "She's my sister." When Abimelek saw Isaac and Rebekah kissing, he called Isaac out and said, "Why did you say that? One of our men could have kissed her and brought great trouble to our land!"

Abimelek told everyone to not harm this family, and Isaac planted crops. God blessed Isaac.

Meanwhile, Esau also married at age forty, but he married into an enemy family. This was a source of grief for Isaac and Rebekah.

On his deathbed, Isaac reached out for Esau nonetheless and asked for that tasty meal Esau always hunted and prepared. This could be his last meal. Esau went out hunting, but Rebecca schemed to get Jacob the blessing. She told Jacob to get a couple goats and she would make Isaac's favorite meal. She wanted Jacob to pretend he was Esau.

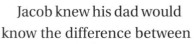

Jacob knew his dad would know the difference between the two sons even if he was going blind. Esau was hairy and had a certain smell. No problem, Rebecca said. "Take that goatskin and put it on your arm. Then go and put on Esau's clothes so you smell like him."

Rebekah made Isaac's favorite dish and Jacob served it wearing Esau's clothes and the goatskin on his arm. Isaac loved the meal, but he became suspicious. "You sound like Jacob, but you're hairy and you smell like Esau." Convinced, Isaac blessed him.

"May God bless you with heavenly and earthly blessings. May nations serve you. May those who curse you, be cursed." A blessing like that from a father gave Jacob full ownership of the family, fulfilling God's promise that the younger would be the boss of the older.

Esau came home and realized Jacob had tricked them. It was too late. Isaac's words could not be taken back. Esau pleaded for a blessing, but Isaac could only say, "You'll live by the sword and serve Jacob." Esau was steaming mad and planned to kill Jacob, so Jacob ran away to Rebekah's brother Laban's house and maybe he could find a wife there.

Jacob's Dysfunctional Family (GENESIS 28–36)

During his journey, Jacob stopped for the night in Bethel, pulled up a rock as his pillow, and had a dream about a huge staircase going from the earth to the heavens. Angels traveled up and down the stairs.

God spoke to Jacob and said, "I'm the God of your grandfather and father. I will give you this land one day and it will be filled with your descendants. You'll be back here." Jacob woke and called that place awesome. He vowed to return.

Jacob traveled to Paddan Aram and met a beautiful girl named Rachel. He discovered she was Laban's daughter. They kissed and went to Laban to ask to be married. Laban wanted Jacob to work for his daughter. Jacob agreed to work for seven years. When the time was up, Jacob said, "It's wedding time!"

But Laban had another daughter, Leah, who couldn't find anyone to marry. She was the older daughter, who, as was custom, usually married first. Laban had promised a marriage to his daughter, but he tricked Jacob into marrying Leah, not Rachel.

Angrily, Jacob confronted Laban. "You gave me the wrong daughter!" Laban did it on purpose, wanting to marry Leah off, but promised to give Jacob Rachel if he worked another seven years. Jacob agreed. The trickster had been tricked.

Leah gave birth to four boys in a row—Reuben, Simeon, Levi, and Judah. Then she stopped having children and wasn't able to have any more, so Rachel's servant, Bilhah, did the substitute thing and gave birth to Dan and Naphtali, whom Rachel claimed as her own. Leah did the same thing as Rachel and gave her servant, Zilpah, to Jacob, and Zilpah gave birth to two more children—Gad and Asher.

Leah suddenly was able to have children again and gave birth to Issachar, Zebulun, and their first daughter, Dinah. God remembered Rachel and allowed her to birth her own baby—Joseph.

Jacob became a master goat breeder, growing his flock quickly. He became very successful, so much so that he

didn't need Laban anymore. Jacob packed up all the women and kids, then headed out. Laban tried to stop him, but it did no good.

Jacob sent word to Esau, hoping they could be brothers again. Esau marched toward Jacob with four hundred men—an army! Jacob split everyone up, expecting an attack.

> Jacob called the place Peniel, which means "face of God," because he saw God face-to-face there.

One night, Jacob sat alone at the fire when a man showed up. They wrestled all night. The man couldn't overpower Jacob, so he touched the socket of Jacob's hip, crippling him. This man was God in human form.

The Lord asked, "What is your name?"

"Jacob," he replied.

"Well, not anymore. Your name is Israel because you struggled with God and came out alive." Because of that fight, Jacob walked with a limp.

Jacob looked up and saw Esau and his army coming. As Jacob prepared for battle, Esau ran to Jacob and hugged him, so happy to see him and meet the whole family. That was unexpected. They spoke and met each other's wives, then went their separate ways. Esau's family line had many descendants who later became Israel's most feared enemies.

Bethlehem means "house of bread." Jesus, who was born in Bethlehem, will call himself "the bread of life."

Later, God appeared to Jacob and confirmed his new name and the nation that would come from him. With all these children, many generations could come from them. Rachel provided one more son to the collection—Benjamin. However, his birth took a toll on Rachel and she died. Jacob buried her in Bethlehem (which would become a very important little town much later).

Isaac also died, at the age of 178 years old, and Esau and Jacob buried him.

Hey, Joe (GENESIS 37-39)

Out of all his sons, Jacob really liked Joseph the most. Joseph always tattled on his brothers, telling Jacob what they did and said. Jacob showed his love to Joseph by making him a wonderful, multicolored robe. That made the brothers hate him even more.

Joseph had wild dreams, and he would tell everyone about them and what they meant.

"I had a dream I was a bundle of hay, and when I stood up, you all bowed to me. I had another dream where the sun, moon, and eleven stars bowed to me."

His brothers got steamed. "Do you think we're all going to bow to you?! No way!"

One day, when Joseph wandered down to see what his brothers were up to, they saw him coming and decided to kill him, telling their father a ferocious animal ate him. Reuben stopped them and said, "Let's not take the poor kid's life."

The brothers didn't kill Joseph. They only attacked him, stripped his robe off, and threw him into an empty, underground watering hole. A caravan of traders came by, and the brothers sold Joseph to them. Then they killed a goat and threw its blood on Joseph's multicolored robe and showed their father, telling him some story about a wild animal attacking and killing Joseph.

Jacob mourned deeply, weeping for days.

Meanwhile, the slave traders took Joseph to Egypt and sold him to one of Pharaoh's officials—a captain of the guards whose name was Potiphar. Potiphar could feel the blessing in his house ever since Joseph joined the staff. He gave

Joseph more and more responsibility until pretty much everything was under Joseph's management.

Joseph was really handsome and well-built. Potiphar's wife noticed him and wanted him badly. One time, she grabbed him and tried to kiss him, but Joseph said, "No, your husband trusts me with everything, even you. I cannot sin against him and God." He ran away but left his cloak in her hand.

Offended, Potiphar's wife got revenge on Joseph and told her husband he tried to take advantage of her. Potiphar threw Joseph in prison. But God was with Joseph in prison. The warden had seen that things started to go more smoothly since Joseph showed up, and he gave Joseph more responsibility until he nearly ran the prison.

The Dreamer (GENESIS 40-41)

Two others were also in prison, both former employees of Pharaoh. One was a cupbearer (a guy who tasted Pharaoh's drinks to make sure they weren't poisoned), and the other a baker. Both had a dream on the same night, and neither dream made any sense. Joseph told them to tell him their dreams, since he had dreams all the time and they made sense to him.

The cupbearer's dream had a vine with three branches that blossomed into grapes. Joseph said in three days he would be released and sent back to work. The baker's dream included three baskets of bread, and birds were eating them out of one basket on his head. Joseph said in three days, Pharaoh would kill him.

In three days, Pharaoh celebrated his birth, releasing the cupbearer and killing the baker, just as Joseph said.

Two years later, Pharaoh had two strange dreams. He saw seven cows, healthy and fat, grazing on grass, while seven other cows, skinny and ugly, came out of the Nile and ate the seven healthy cows. In his other dream, he saw seven healthy heads of grain swallowed up by seven thin and burnt heads of grain.

Pharaoh cried out for someone to make sense of those dreams. The cupbearer remembered, "There was this guy in prison, Joseph. He in-terprets dreams."

They brought Joseph to Pharaoh. Pharaoh asked Joseph to tell him what the dreams meant.

Joseph said, "I can't tell you what it means, but God can." Joseph said, "The seven healthy cows and seven good heads of grain represent seven years of abundant crops. The seven sick cows and seven ugly heads of grain represent seven years of famine that will follow the seven good years. You need to build up a sur-plus of grain during the seven good years to prepare for the seven bad years."

Pharaoh understood and put Joseph in charge of everything, elevating him from prisoner to second-in-command. At thirty years old, Joseph got married and had two sons, Manasseh and Ephraim. He managed Egypt during the good times, and they stored up tons of grain to prepare for the bad. When the bad times arrived, they were ready.

Meet the Israels (GENESIS 42–50)

Meanwhile, Joseph's father and brothers suffered during the famine. They heard Egypt had tons of food. Jacob told ten of his sons (not Benjamin) to go to Egypt and buy some grain. They arrived in Egypt and the brothers bowed down to Joseph, whom they didn't recognize (just like Joseph's dream said they wouldn't).

Joseph recognized them, calling them spies. He demanded they tell the truth. They told him all about their family, including their youngest brother, Benjamin. "Then go get him," said Joseph, "but one of you must stay here in prison."

The brothers talked amongst themselves. "You see, all these bad things are happening because of what we did to Joseph." Joseph heard them, fighting back tears. Simeon was chosen to stay in prison.

Joseph had their donkeys loaded with grain, but he also returned the silver they gave as payment. On their way home, the brothers found the silver and cried out, "What is God doing to us!"

> Many times in Genesis, people went to Egypt for help and protection. Joseph, Mary, and Jesus will also go to Egypt to hide while Herod seeks to kill the newborns.

They arrived at their father's house and told him the story. He yelled at his boys, saying, "First Joseph, then Simeon, and now you want to take away Benjamin! No way! You can't take my youngest son!"

Over time, they ate all the grain they received from Egypt and had to go back. They remembered what the Egyptian official said. When they returned, they had to bring Benjamin. Jacob didn't like it, but Judah promised they would bring back Benjamin safely.

Joseph greeted them and heard about their father, Jacob, still alive and well. He saw his younger brother Benjamin and wanted to cry. Joseph slipped away and hid his tears. Then he provided dinner for them, and Benjamin got five times the amount of food compared to the others.

As the brothers prepared to go, Joseph had a servant stash his favorite silver cup in Benjamin's bag. Along their trip back, Joseph's servant rode out and stopped them, stating that a favorite silver cup of his master's was missing. When it was found in Benjamin's bag, he was arrested and taken back to Egypt.

The brothers freaked and begged for Benjamin's release. "It will kill our father if we don't return with him." Joseph couldn't stand it any longer. He cried out to his brothers, "I am Joseph!" They couldn't believe it. As they got closer, they realized he was telling the truth.

Joseph explained what happened, giving all credit to God. They hugged it out and cried like babies. Joseph gave them a bunch of money and supplies to return home and get their dad, demanding they bring him to Egypt, where Joseph would take care of them.

Jacob heard the news and praised God. God came to Jacob in a dream and said, "Don't be afraid to go to Egypt. I'll bring your people back one day." They packed up all the families—sixty-six people total—and moved to Egypt, in an area known as Goshen.

Jacob and Joseph saw each other, and hugged and cried. Joseph told them to say they were shepherds and the Egyptians would leave them alone. Egyptians put shepherds at the bottom of the social scale.

As the famine grew throughout the region, many nations came to Egypt for grain just as Joseph had strategized. This made Egypt very wealthy. The plan God worked through Joseph saved many lives.

Jacob lived in Egypt for seventeen more years, then got very ill. He asked, before he died, to not be buried in Egypt but with his ancestors in Abraham's cave in Machpelah. Joseph agreed.

Joseph brought his sons, Ephraim and Manasseh, to Jacob to be blessed. He did, technically bringing them into the family. Then Jacob blessed all his sons. For some, he had good things to say. For others, not so good.

The best blessing was for Judah. A prophecy. He called him a lion's cub who will hold a scepter, like a king. Jacob then spoke of a donkey and a colt and robes of blood.

Jacob finished his blessing and died at the age of 147 years. Joseph and all of Egypt mourned his passing. Joseph and all his brothers got Pharaoh's permission to go to Machpelah and bury Jacob. They then all returned to Egypt.

Once back, the brothers got nervous now that Jacob was gone. They were afraid Joseph would get back at them for the whole robe thing.

Joseph overheard them and said, "Don't worry. You wanted to hurt me, but God intended good to come out of it, saving many lives along the way."

> Two thousand years later, Jesus would come from the line of Judah, riding a donkey and a colt into Jerusalem to be crucified, his robe covered in blood.

Later on, Joseph was ready to die. He asked that when they leave one day, that they carry his bones in a coffin back home. Joseph died at the age of 110.

A lot of time passes—like four hundred years—until the story picks back up, this time with Moses.

WHAT'S THE POINT?

▸ Abraham showed a lot of faith, trusting God to work through him.

▸ Jacob called Judah a lion and a king. The phrase "Lion of Judah" and "King of kings" comes from that description. Even this early in Genesis, God was preparing the world for Jesus.

▸ The name *Israel* means "God strives." The name change implies that God would now fight for Israel and his descendants. The name change fits the radical transformation of Jacob.

▸ When bad things happen, it may lead to something good, even if for decades nothing good seems to come from it.

3

Moses and the Exodus

EXODUS 1-15

WHO'S WHO

- » **Moses**—the youngest child of three
- » **Aaron**—the older brother
- » **Miriam**—the middle sister
- » **Pharaoh's daughter**—adopts a baby found in a river
- » **Moses' mom**—dropped off one of her kids at the Nile
- » **Pharaoh**—don't tell him . . . but he's not God
- » **Reuel/Jethro**—Moses' father-in-law
- » **Zipporah**—Moses' wife
- » **Gershom**—Moses' firstborn son

WHERE ARE WE?

- » **Egypt**—where we left Joseph and Jacob's family four hundred years ago, shepherding sheep in a region called Goshen near the Nile River

INTERESTING STUFF IN THIS SECTION

» The Nile River flows south to north; all other rivers in the northern hemisphere flow north to south.

» "Exodus" means an exit or mass departure.

» Each of the plagues showed a different aspect of God's power over the gods the Egyptians worshiped, including water, amphibians, insects, mammals, precipitation, bacteria, the sun, then finally life or death.

» The name of the Red Sea is actually "Reed Sea."

From Bad to Worse (EXODUS 1)

When we last left the Israelites (the family of Jacob renamed Israel), they lived in Egypt under the protection of Pharaoh because of Joseph's plan that saved the nation during a severe famine. Everybody loved Joseph and his family.

Over time—like four hundred years—new pharaohs rose to power, and they forgot all the nice things about Joseph and the Israelites. In fact, Israelites were looked at as outsiders who were becoming a threat because of their increasing population.

Egypt decided to make Israelites their slaves; the masters worked them harshly and ruthlessly.

Then the king of Egypt came up with another idea. He told the Hebrew nurses who helped with the births of babies to kill all the newborn boys. These women, also known as midwives, refused, telling Pharaoh that the

Hebrew women gave birth before they showed up, and certainly he didn't want them to kill the already born babies!

He did, and he made it a rule to throw all the living baby boys into the Nile. (Girls could live.)

Mo-Mo-Moses Boat, Gently Down the Stream
(EXODUS 2–3)

A Levite man married a Levite woman, and a son was born. But with all the rules Pharaoh put into place, Mommy hid the baby for three months, then put him in a basket and floated him down the Nile. Pharaoh's daughter was relaxing by the riverbanks when she saw the basket passing by. When she looked inside, she thought the Nile was sending her a gift, so she pulled the baby out and called him Moses, which means "pulled out of the water." Moses' sister, Miriam, saw what happened and

told Pharoah's daughter to hire a Hebrew woman she knew to take care of the baby. Guess what—that Hebrew woman was Moses' mom!

Moses lived between Egyptian royalty and Hebrew poverty for forty years. One day he saw an Egyptian beating a Hebrew. Moses stepped in and killed the Egyptian. When word spread about what he did, Moses ran, hiding in a place called Midian, up in the mountains.

Moses, always the superhero, protected seven sisters who were being harassed by a gang of shepherds around a well. The women took him home to their father, Reuel (also known as Jethro), and he gave Moses one of his daughters, Zipporah, in marriage. Moses went into the shepherding business for the next forty years. He had his first son, named Gershom.

Meanwhile, back in Egypt, the Israelites cried out for God to help them because of all the slave labor they were being made to do. God heard their cry and began to put a plan together.

The Talking Bush (EXODUS 4)

Moses tended his flocks on a mountain named Horeb when a bush caught fire and a voice spoke to him.

"Moses, Moses, I am the God of Abraham, Isaac, and Jacob. I see the misery of my people in Egypt. I'm here to save them. I will take them out of Egypt and send them to a beautiful place north of here. And you'll be the one who leads them."

Everything sounded good to Moses, up to that last part. "Me? Who am I? And who are you again?"

"My name is *I am*. The Lord. The God of your fathers. Now, go and tell the Israelite elders that God said for everyone to take a three-day trip to the wilderness to worship God. When you ask Pharaoh for permission, he won't like it. But I'll do some marvelous things and he'll give in. In fact, they'll pay you to leave!"

Moses wondered, "What if they don't believe me?" God told Moses to throw his staff to the ground, and it turned into a snake. Moses touched the snake and it turned back into a staff. Then God told Moses to put his hand in his cloak and pull it out. It was covered in a skin disease called leprosy. When Moses put his hand back in his cloak and pulled it out, the leprosy was gone. "How's that for proof?"

Moses responded with another excuse. "Yeah, but I'm not very good with public speaking. My words get all twisted. Send someone else."

God wasn't happy with this. "Fine, I'll send your brother, Aaron, along with you to do all the talking."

Running out of excuses, Moses went to Egypt once all those people who wanted him dead were dead. He brought Aaron up to speed about what God said to him, then told the leaders of the Israelites what God wanted to do. A huge worship service broke out.

Hard-Hearted Pharaoh (EXODUS 5–6)

Everything seemed good until Moses and Aaron went to Pharaoh and said these words: "God says, let my people go."

Pharaoh thought he was God, so the idea of another God telling him what to do was not normal. Moses outlined the three-day spiritual retreat they wanted to take to the wilderness to offer up sacrifices. Pharaoh immediately thought, *These people obviously have too much time on their hands.* He ordered the slave drivers to have the Israelites make their own bricks from scratch and make more of them daily.

Moses went to God. "Why did you make me do this? All I do is cause trouble."

God replied, "I am God. I will save these people. They will be my people and I will be their God!"

Moses went and told this to the people, but they were too busy and upset to listen.

God said to Moses, "Pharaoh is a tough man, but I'll make his heart very difficult, and then you'll see what I can do."

So now, in their eighties, Moses and Aaron went back again to Pharaoh. Aaron threw down his staff and it became a snake. Pharaoh had a bunch of wise men, magicians, and sorcerers. They took a staff and did the same thing. But Aaron's snake swallowed their snakes.

There were more miracles to come.

Here Come the Plagues (EXODUS 7–10)

God told Moses to tell Pharaoh to let his people go or he'll turn the Nile into blood. Pharaoh said no, so Moses struck his staff to the water and it turned to blood. Pharaoh's magicians also turned water to blood. Moses was just doing magic tricks, they all thought. No one was impressed except for the fact that their main drinking source just became undrinkable.

For the second miracle, Moses asked Pharaoh again to let the Israelites go or God will cause a flood of frogs to infest the land. Pharaoh denied them, so God allowed frogs to appear everywhere, coming out of the water and out of the land. The magicians did a similar trick, and everyone shrugged—no big deal. But there were frogs as far as they could see, in every courtyard and every house, at kitchen tables, in beds and bathrooms. Then the frogs died and the place stunk!

Pharaoh wouldn't budge. Aaron raised his staff and swarms of gnats poured over the land. The magicians tried this trick but couldn't follow—big fail!

But Pharaoh still wouldn't budge. God then allowed flies to buzz by the billions everywhere, except around the Israelites.

Pharaoh budged slightly and allowed them to go, but changed his mind once the flies left. Five plagues down. Five to go.

A sickness struck the livestock next, getting the Egyptian cows, sheep, and goats sick, but not the Israelites' livestock. Pharaoh still said no.

Then God allowed a plague of boils—painful pimples—to appear on people's bodies. Only the Egyptians got the boils. Not the Israelites. Pharaoh still said no.

Next came a hailstorm of gigantic ice rocks falling from the sky. Despite being given a warning, the Egyptians left their livestock and their servants out, all of which got killed, and all the crops flattened. The Israelites were just fine, though.

This time Pharaoh called himself a sinner! "The Lord is right and I'm wrong! Pray for me, Moses! Yes, you can go!" But once the thunder and hail stopped, Pharaoh changed his mind again and told them to stay.

The same thing happened with swarms and swarms of locusts, eating up every plant in sight. Pharaoh did the same thing as last time—cried for mercy but changed his mind once the plague left.

Then God put all of Egypt into darkness (except where the Israelites lived, where the sun shone bright and clear). For three days, the Egyptians could not see their hand in front of their face. Pharaoh said, "Go!" then said, "No!"

Nine down. One to go.

Pass Us Over, Death (EXODUS 11–12)

God had one last plague in his arsenal. This was a biggie: Every firstborn son in Egypt would die.

To prevent that from happening to them, the Israelites needed to sacrifice a year-old lamb without any defect on the tenth day of the month and spread the lamb's blood on the sides and on the top of their doors. When the angel of death came to strike down the houses, he would see the blood that marked and covered the house, and no one would be killed inside. Death would literally "pass over" the house.

Then, they were given very specific instructions about how to eat the lamb and the entire Passover meal. The bread had to be made without yeast (like a cracker) because they would not have time to wait for it to rise. This later led to a celebration called the Festival of Unleavened Bread, and later, Passover. In the future, it was a day to remind the Israelites of this awesome event.

At midnight, after the Israelites did what God asked, the angel of death struck down all the firstborn, including Pharaoh's son. Terrible wailing and crying was heard all throughout the night.

Pharaoh brought Moses and Aaron before him and said, "Leave us! Go! Take what you want and get out!" They grabbed whatever they needed and asked the Egyptians for their gold and silver. The Egyptians paid them to get out, just as God promised.

About 600,000 Israelite men (with women and children it was over a million people) walked out of Egypt that night. They had lived in Egypt for 430 years.

Taking a Walk through the Sea (EXODUS 13-15:21)

As the Israelites walked away, Moses remembered to take Joseph's bones (his last wish) with them to be buried in the Promised Land.

God guided them with a pillar of smoke by day and a pillar of light by night.

Right about this time, Pharaoh realized he lost and said, "What were we thinking? Let's get those guys!" They loaded up their chariots and chased the Israelites. The Israelites saw what was ahead of them—a huge sea, called the Red Sea, and the Egyptian army coming up behind them. They were trapped!

The people yelled at Moses, "You brought us out here to die! You should have left us in Egypt!"

Moses yelled back, "Don't panic! God will save us!"

And he did. God told Moses to raise his staff, and the Red Sea opened up, creating a road through it. It opened with just enough time for all the Israelites to walk through to the other side, but closed just as the Egyptians in their chariots tried to cross. The whole Egyptian army drowned.

The people trusted Moses as their leader at that time. They also feared the Lord and his power. Moses sang a song and so did his sister, Miriam.

Setting out on their walk across the desert wilderness, they needed water. They found a pool, which they called Marah, because the water was bitter.

Every time the Israelites complained, God graciously provided to meet their needs. He did this out of love. But the people would soon push God too far.

WHAT'S THE POINT?

- God will do whatever it takes to save his people and free them. He would go so far as to send his Son to earth to die and free us from our sins.

- God will call people to help him save other people. You could be a leader to help save people.

- You may think you're not a good speaker or a smart leader, but God will show you and even bring others in to help you.

Wilderness Time

EXODUS 15:22–40:38

WHO'S WHO

» **Moses**—he gets to see God face-to-face and has the suntan to prove it

» **Aaron**—promoted to high priest, but makes a huge mistake the size of a cow

» **Reuel/Jethro**—Moses' father-in-law, who has some good advice

» **Joshua**—Moses' army commander; being groomed to replace Moses one day

WHERE ARE WE?

» **Wilderness**—there's not much food and water in a wilderness, but God still provided.

» **Mount Sinai**—God spent more time on this mountain than any other mountain in the world.

INTERESTING STUFF IN THIS SECTION

» Moses spent two forty-day experiences with God on the mountain. He was told a lot of information and compiled it into a book.

» Mount Sinai is probably in the Egyptian Sinai Peninsula. We don't know which mountain precisely was Mount Sinai, but different people have pointed out ones that seem likely.

» God's laws speak about how to handle kidnappings, what to do if someone's bull kills a person, and what kind of payment should happen if you are baby-sitting someone's donkey and it dies.

» God does not like sorceresses.

» The tabernacle was made with curtains and curtain rods, just like your shower curtain, but hundreds of times bigger.

» The "Promised Land" is the area we call Israel. God promised the Israelites that he would take them to this land and give it to them.

Grumblers (EXODUS 15:22–19:25)

It didn't take long for the people to forget all the great things God had done, when they walked up to a pool of water and discovered the water was bitter. They cried, "Great, now we're going to die of thirst." God told Moses to toss a piece of wood into the water, and the water was purified, ready to drink.

Then the people grumbled about their diet. God provided quail.

As the Israelites traveled from Elim to the Desert of Sin, the whole community started to grumble against Moses and Aaron. They wanted to die in Egypt instead of dying in the desert from lack of food.

When the Israelites woke up the next morning, it literally rained bread from the sky. God had answered them by providing thin, frost-like flakes that fell from the sky. It tasted just like honey and coriander-seed bread. They gathered the flakey substance, enough for one day, but they had to trust that God would provide more the next day and not take too much. If they did, the stuff they stored would be covered in maggots. The only time they could take more than enough was the day before the Sabbath, since God didn't want them working that day.

> When the people looked at it, they said, "What is it?" That's what it was called—*what is it*—which translated in the Hebrew language is the word *manna*.

God supplied exactly what they needed in the desert—fresh bread every morning called manna. God told Moses to keep a jar of manna to show future generations what he miraculously did.

53

You would think the manna incident would make the people trust God for help, but it didn't. Again, they complained about water. "We're going to die of thirst!"

God patiently heard them and answered, telling Moses to strike his staff against a rock at Mount Horeb. Moses did and water gushed out.

Their next enemy—the Amalekites—attacked them, ready for war. Moses sent his trusted army commander, Joshua, out to fight, while Moses stood on a mountain with his arms raised by his side. When his arms were up, the Israelites were winning. When his arms dropped, the Amalekites were winning. Aaron and Hur stepped in and held Moses' arms up until the Israelites won!

Moses stayed very busy as the leader and ultimate decision maker, listening to complaints from people and acting as a judge in disputes. It filled his calendar from morning to night.

One day, Moses' father-in-law, Jethro, came by to see Zipporah, his daughter, and the grandkids. Moses and Zipporah had since had another child, named Eliezer. Moses caught Jethro up on all that had happened. Jethro was impressed, but when he saw how busy Moses was all day, he was concerned.

"You can't go running around like this all the time. You need to pick some capable men who fear God and are trustworthy and not greedy, and appoint them as officials over different groups. If you do this, it will take a huge pressure off your back."

Moses did and it worked great! He gave the officials the easier cases while he took on the toughest cases.

Ten Commandments Mountain (EXODUS 20)

The Israelites arrived at Mount Sinai and camped right at the foot of the mountain. Moses went up to talk to God at the top of Mount Sinai.

God said, "Tell the people if they obey everything I tell them to do, I will love them more than any other nation. They will be a kingdom of priests and a holy nation."

The people agreed and said they would do whatever God wanted. God told them to wash up and not to touch the mountain because it would become holy ground.

Moses went up the mountain. Smoke covered the mountaintop. The ground trembled. Trumpets blared. The Lord actually showed up on Mount Sinai and spoke to Moses. He started by laying out the Ten Commandments,

which God etched on two tablets of stone with his own finger. They were:

1. Don't have any other gods besides me.
2. Don't make any images or idols and worship them.
3. Don't misuse the name of God.
4. Remember the Sabbath and keep it special.
5. Honor your mother and father.
6. Don't murder.
7. Don't commit adultery.
8. Don't steal.
9. Don't lie about your neighbor.
10. Don't envy the things your neighbor has.

Forty Days, Forty Nights, Part 1 (EXODUS 21–31)

God then laid out a number of important laws he wanted this holy nation to live by. These rules covered how to treat your servants, what to do when you injure someone, what to do if your animal injures someone, how to protect your property, and even laws about borrowing other people's things.

During this time, God also gave a principle known by us today: the "eye for an eye, tooth for a tooth" system for justice. It says if you poke out someone's eye, your eye should get poked out. If you knock out someone's tooth, your tooth should get knocked out. It speaks of justice equal to the crime.

God really emphasized those rules about not worshiping other gods. He knew how dangerous it could be when people got distracted by idols and started following false gods.

God promised that an angel would go ahead of them and make a way, weakening those enemies in the land he promised them. He made it clear to never make any promises with those people or their gods.

When Moses repeated all these rules and promises to the people, they all happily cried, "We will do everything the Lord has commanded!"

Moses returned to the mountain as smoke covered it. He stayed there, this time for forty days and nights.

During that long period of time, God covered a lot of valuable information with Moses. Specifically, God outlined how the tabernacle would work. In those areas were utensils and fixtures (tables, lamps, altars) used for the sacrifices and worship. God gave two men, Bezalel and Oholiab, special wisdom and skills to build everything precisely according to God's will.

> The tabernacle was a portable worship center made of pipe and drape, with places for worship and sacrifices. It was a model for the future temple.

On the ground, Moses met God in a place called a Tent of Meeting. When he went in, the people stood. When he came out, the people listened to what God told Moses to say.

The ark of the covenant was a very special container, made of wood, covered with gold, fastened with rings so it could be carried with poles. It was a very holy piece that could not be touched. Inside, this ark (which means a container that holds things) would hold the tablets with the Ten Commandments and a jar of manna.

God also designed the garments that the priests wore. The priests were from the line of Levi, one of Jacob's twelve sons, so they were called Levites, and it included Aaron and Moses. Aaron would be the first high priest. The garments displayed lots of images to remind the priests why they were performing the sacrifices. The priests' role was to stand between sinful people and a holy God and perform the sacrifices needed to provide forgiveness. A ceremony was given to purify the priests and set them apart for their very special job.

On the Jewish calendar, the Sabbath was a Saturday. When Jesus rose again from the dead on a Sunday, Christians changed that day of worship and reflection to Sunday.

The Sabbath was very important to God—so important that God said anyone who did not honor it would be put to death. It was not only a day of rest for the people, but a day of reflection and connection with God. It was a day to trust in God by not working and providing for oneself. The Sabbath was modeled after the seventh day of rest that God engaged in when he created the world.

That Golden Cow (EXODUS 32)

While Moses got all this valuable information on the mountaintop, the people down below got scared. "Where's Moses?"

The people returned to their old Egyptian ways and said, "Hey, let's make a golden calf and worship that!"

Aaron, who should have known better, answered by taking up all their golden earrings, melting them down, and making a golden calf. "Here's your god who brought you up out of Israel!" Just like that, they broke commandments one and two.

While the people partied, God said to Moses, "You had better get back to the people. They are out of their minds and I'm getting really mad at them."

Moses came down with the Ten Commandments, saw what they were doing, and smashed the stone tablets. He took the golden calf and burned it in the fire.

He turned to his brother. "Aaron, how could you allow this to happen?"

Aaron lied. "These people are so evil. They forced me to do it. I threw the gold jewelry into the fire and this golden calf jumped out!"

Moses gathered the Levites and armed them with swords. He told them to walk the camp and kill anyone who loved this god. They did, and three thousand died.

Moses stood before the people and told them God was really angry at them. Moses was going to go to the Lord, who hopefully would forgive them. Moses pleaded with God. God would forgive, but first they needed to be punished. A great plague struck the people.

Forty Days, Forty Nights, Part 2 (EXODUS 33-40)

Returning to the mountain, Moses asked to see God's glory. God replied, "No one sees my face and lives, but if you stand behind this rock, I'll give you a glimpse." God then told Moses to chisel out two more stone tablets and give that Ten Commandments thing another try. God gave Moses more important rules to follow and sent him back to the people. That was Moses' second forty-day encounter with God.

When Moses showed up, people could tell he had been with God. His face was glowing so much he had to put a veil over it!

Moses told the people what God said, and they all went to work to build the tabernacle God wanted. Bezalel and Oholiab supervised many skilled people. Moses asked people to bring materials for the construction, and they brought all they had—so much that Moses had to tell them to stop giving!

The tabernacle, ark of the covenant, and all the utensils used for worship and sacrifice were assembled, including the priestly garments for the Levites.

Once it was all done, Moses looked at their work. It was perfect, done exactly as God wanted. Moses set it all up and a cloud covered the Tent of Meeting as the glory of the Lord showed up and filled the tabernacle. It was so powerful, Moses had to step away.

God showed his approval by being there with them. Soon, though, God will wish he never brought these people out of Egypt.

WHAT'S THE POINT?

► God does not want us worshiping or putting our trust in any god but him. He loves us so much; other gods will only hurt us.

► There are many sins listed in the Bible. All sins are really the same. A sin is when we do something God doesn't want us to do.

► The Ten Commandments are in two categories— sins against God (1–4) and sins against other people (5–10). That's why Jesus said the greatest commandment was to love God and love people. Those two rules sum up all the Ten Commandments.

► We must trust God even when it looks like things are impossible or hopeless. He loves you and he will take care of you.

5

Forty Years Later

LEVITICUS; NUMBERS; AND DEUTERONOMY

WHO'S WHO

» **Moses**—he throws a temper tantrum and loses his Promised Land card

» **Joshua**—gets chosen to lead after Moses dies

» **Caleb**—a man of faith and a real tough guy

WHERE ARE WE?

» **Mount Sinai**—time to leave the mountain and face many more mountains

» **Wilderness**—a nice place to visit, but you wouldn't want to live there

» **Mount Nebo**—a big mountain on the border of Jordan overlooking Israel, where Moses died

INTERESTING STUFF IN THIS SECTION

» The book of Leviticus gets its name because the book applied to the Levite priests.

» The book of Numbers gets its name because God asked for all the people to be counted.

» The book of Deuteronomy means "second law," because Moses covered all the information in the law a second time for a new generation.

» The first five books of the Bible are called "The Law." They cover God's law for mankind.

» The term "a land flowing with milk and honey" means that the animals are healthy and producing milk, and the bees are pollinating the flowers and trees. The ecosystem is in perfect balance.

» Moses' life is broken down in three sections of forty: forty years in Egypt, forty years as a shepherd in Midian, forty years leading the Israelites to the Promised Land.

Levi Genes (LEVITICUS)

If someone was born in the line of Levi, they qualified to be a priest and took part in the sacrificial system. During the time of Moses, all those sacrifices happened in a portable temple, called a tabernacle. In the time of Solomon, it would happen, finally, in a permanent structure called a temple.

God had very specific information he wanted the Levites to know about a number of topics, such as the different types of sacrifices, the many festivals or celebrations, and very specific rules that helped someone live a holy life. Sometimes that information seemed gross and yucky, but God knows that people live in a world that's gross and yucky. He told them what needed to be said.

Count Off (NUMBERS 1-10)

A year and a month had passed since the Israelites left Egypt. That's when God told Moses to take a census, counting all the people and dividing up the leadership into groups. They counted every male who was twenty years and older—those old enough to serve in God's army. The number came to 603,550. The Levites weren't counted in that number because they did not serve in the army, but rather in the tabernacle.

Then God asked that the tribes be organized when they settled in a camp around the tabernacle (which contained the ark of the covenant). The tribes were assembled in a circle around the tabernacle in the center. The Levites' job was to disassemble, carry, and reassemble the tabernacle whenever God moved them.

God covered many more rules with them regarding marriage, purity, vows, and offerings.

Since a year had passed, it was time for the second Passover. God then had Moses make two silver trumpets that would call people to assemble, to celebrate, and to go to war.

God was ready to move them, so the pillar of smoke that they'd been following lifted off the tabernacle at their home base in Mount Sinai. They packed up and followed. The ark of the covenant was carried at the front of the procession.

More Complaints and Grumblings
(NUMBERS 11–19)

The people grumbled about all this hardship. God had enough, so he brought fire down from the sky and killed the grumblers.

Then a group started grumbling about not having food other than manna all the time. Even Moses couldn't stand the complaining any longer. God blew in so much quail that it covered the whole camp. The people snatched up all they could, but there was something about their attitude that made God mad. So he struck them with a severe plague.

As they traveled to a new location, this time Miriam and Aaron joined the complaining against their brother, Moses. God called them to the front office—the Tent of Meeting. After his scolding of them, Miriam's skin turned white as snow (leprosy). Moses cried out for God to stop, and he did. Miriam was healed.

The Israelites moved some more, closing in on the land promised them. God made sure each tribe had a specific leader, such as Joshua overseeing the tribe of Ephraim and Caleb, being the leader of the tribe of Judah. God told those twelve leaders to cross over into the Promised

Land, spy on the people who were there, and bring back a report.

Forty days later, the spies returned, excited, saying the land was great with lots of stuff growing. They even brought a bunch of fruit to prove it.

But . . .

They also reported that the people who lived there were huge, powerful, strong warriors. Ten of the tribal leaders shook their heads. "No way we can ever beat them in a fight."

Joshua and Caleb disagreed. "We can take that land because God's on our side!"

The people only listened to the ten whiners. They got so scared, they tried to figure out a way to return to Egypt. Moses and Aaron pleaded with the people not to think that way. Then Moses turned to God, asking for forgiveness.

God said, "I forgive them, but none of them will enter that Promised Land. In fact, it will be forty years from now—one year for every day the spies were gone—when I'll open up the Promised Land. That's just enough time for this faithless generation to die."

The ten who gave the bad report were killed by a plague. The people mourned, then decided to enter the Promised Land on their own, to show that they were ready. But an army of Amalekites and Canaanites beat them back. They were doomed to die in the desert and never see the Promised Land with their own eyes—all except Joshua and Caleb, the only two who trusted God.

Another rebellion broke out, this time with a Levite family headed by a man named Korah, and 250 other men. God told them to assemble, then told everyone else to step back. Moses cried out for mercy, but God said he had to punish grumblers. The ground opened up and swallowed Korah's family, while fire burned up the grumblers.

God's wrath burned hotter against the people. A plague killed thousands until Moses stepped in again, pleading for God to stop. God listened to Moses and the plague ended.

But that did not stop the people from complaining. Another argument broke out and God wanted to make sure they understood that Aaron and the Levites were the chosen priests. God asked every tribal leader to bring their own personal staff, write their name on it, and set it before the ark of the covenant. "The tribe belonging to the staff that buds and blossoms overnight is the tribe of my chosen priests."

When they went the next morning and looked at the dead branches the men used as walking sticks, only Aaron's staff had budded and blossomed like it was alive.

It even grew almonds! That quieted another argument amongst the people . . . for now. That staff also went into the ark of the covenant.

Moses Gets a Time-Out (NUMBERS 20–21)

Some time had passed. Miriam died and was buried. The Israelites faced a water crisis and began to quarrel with Moses and Aaron.

They moaned and whined, "Oh, if only we had died in Egypt instead of out here in the wilderness. At least there we had grain, figs, and grapes!"

Moses asked God what to do. God said, "Take your staff and speak to the rock in front of the people. Water will pour out."

Moses took his staff and went to the rock. In front of everyone, he lost his cool. "Here you go, you rebels! Here's your water!" He smashed the rock twice with the staff. Water gushed out.

God pulled Moses aside and said, "You didn't trust me or honor me just then, so I'm not allowing you to enter the Promised Land."

Later, Moses sent messengers to Edom and asked if they could pass through their land. They were denied (remember, these are descendants of Esau). This didn't help the relations between the two countries.

God told Moses that his brother, Aaron, would die, and asked that his high priest clothing be given to Aaron's son Eleazar on Mount Hur. All of them went to the mountain. Aaron transferred the clothing to his son, then died.

After a time of mourning for Aaron, the grumblers returned to their grumbling, focusing their displeasure on God and Moses. God responded by sending venomous snakes to them, biting and killing Israelites left and right.

That woke up everyone. "Hey, we have sinned against God, Moses! Stop these snakes!"

God offered an interesting remedy. "Make a bronze snake and put it on a pole. Everyone who looks at it will be healed." It worked, and even if they were bitten, they lived.

Just like people who look to the cross to be saved from their deadly, poisonous sins, the Israelites looked to the bronze snake on a staff. Both situations require faith to be healed.

During that time, Israel enjoyed many successes, winning wars and capturing cities. Word of their strength grew and the kings in the area grew very nervous.

A Prophet and His Talking Donkey
(NUMBERS 22–25)

Meanwhile, as the Israelites grew in power, other kingdoms in the area got nervous, especially King Balak of Moab. They were terrified! He realized they couldn't defeat the Israelites physically, so he decided to go after them spiritually.

Balak sent messengers to hire a prophet to rain down curses on the Israelites. The prophet's name was Balaam. God told Balaam, "Do not go with these people and do not put a curse on my people."

Balaam told Balak no, he wouldn't curse these people for all the silver and gold in the world. But God told Balaam to go with Balak and do only what God told him to do.

Balaam jumped on his favorite donkey and apparently didn't do what God wanted, so God sent an angel to intercept him. The donkey could sense the angel, and he kept going off the path. Balaam could not see the angel and thought the donkey was just being difficult. He beat the donkey three times for disobedience.

That's when the donkey spoke up. "What have I done to you that you beat me three times?"

"You keep making a fool of me!" Balaam replied.

"Have I ever behaved like this before?" the donkey said.

"No."

Then God opened Balaam's eyes and he saw the angel. Balaam bowed, embarrassed. The angel said to Balaam, "The donkey saw me three times and you couldn't see me once. The donkey saved your life because I was going to kill you." Balaam apologized some more. Then the angel said, "Go with these men from Moab, but only say what I tell you."

Balaam told Balak to build seven altars and he would receive a word from the Lord to give to Balak. Balak built those altars and Balaam went to each to get a message. The messages were all pretty much the same—God is great and powerful, and these are his people.

Balak didn't like those messages, so he found a way to seduce the Israelites immorally with his god, Baal. It worked; many male Israelites fell for it.

God's anger burned red hot against the Israelites until one of the priests, Phinehas, killed

> Balaam's fourth message actually contains a prediction of a king being born, and a star out of Jacob signaling his birth. The wise men must have read that verse in Numbers 24:17.

a man about to sin because of this god Baal. That death stopped a terrible plague God unleashed.

Forty-Year Anniversary (NUMBERS 26–36)

Asecond census occurred, marking forty years in the wilderness, counting all the men twenty years and older. The total number of fighting men came to 601,730. This was less than they had counted in the first census.

God told Moses to lay his hands on Joshua. God recognized that Joshua had a spirit of leadership, and he would take over Moses' job when Moses died. Everybody saw this and knew God wanted Joshua to lead after Moses died.

The Israelites took revenge on the Midianites for their role in Balak's plan. Even Balaam was killed, supposedly since he sold out and told Balak how to bring down the Israelites. They divided up the spoils after completely wiping out the towns.

As they approached the Promised Land, three of the tribes—the Reubenites, Gadites, and the tribe from Joseph's son Manasseh—saw the land on the east side of the Jordan River (known today as Jordan) and wanted to live there. Moses allowed them to, as long as the men joined in the war to wipe out the enemies in the Promised Land. After that they could return. The men agreed.

The people looked back over their long journey to get here. They sure visited a lot of places.

Now they looked ahead. That area in Canaan was huge and needed to be divided up by tribes. They needed to build cities for the Levites since they did not inherit any land, only the most important job in Israel as priests. They also came up with cities of refuge—safe towns where people could go until their trial date came up and be free from revenge.

On the Border (DEUTERONOMY)

After many victories over their enemy armies along the way, Moses began to wrap things up on earth. He appointed leaders, commanders, and judges to take care of the people. They sent out spies to check out the Promised Land. They returned, this time with good news, confident they could defeat anyone with God on their side.

Moses began a long, final speech to this new generation of Israelites, forty years after they left Egypt. He went through the history of what got them to this point, the victories, and the agonizing defeats. Moses reminded them about how angry they had made God.

> Jesus quoted two verses from Deuteronomy when tempted in the wilderness by Satan, and cited two quotes from the book as the greatest commandments ever!

He summarized the law, including the Ten Commandments, and gave them another important law: *Love the Lord your God with all your heart and with all your soul and with all your strength.* Moses covered the importance of telling the next generation about God's love and power, and how he provides. He reminded them that people do not live on bread alone, but on every word that comes from God's mouth.

Moses used this time to make sure everyone followed their next leader, Joshua. Then Moses sang a song. He blessed the tribes and climbed Mount Nebo, where God showed him the land that he worked so hard to see but would never set foot in.

Moses died at the age of 120, and God buried him in a secret place. The nation grieved his departure. Up to that time, no one had ever shown so much power or performed such mighty deeds as Moses.

The Spirit of wisdom filled Joshua. He was ready for the next chapter in Israel's history.

WHAT'S THE POINT?

▶ God is patient with us despite our complaining. He has the power to wipe us out but allows us to live.

▶ God has lots of time on his hands. He controls time. Forty years is like a second to him.

▶ Going to the Promised Land is a lot like our journey through this wilderness called life to a place of peace called heaven. God will guide us there, give us wisdom, and protect us from our enemies.

6

We Are the Champions
JOSHUA

WHO'S WHO

» **Joshua**—chosen to lead after Moses died

» **Caleb**—a scrappy old man of faith

» **Rahab**—a questionable woman with an honorable legacy

WHERE ARE WE?

» **Jericho**—a city that used to have these big walls

» **Jerusalem**—this place will become very important later

» **Ai**—another city with the least number of letters in the Bible (Ur the other)

INTERESTING STUFF IN THIS SECTION

» The name *Joshua* comes from the same root word as Jesus, meaning "salvation."

» Rahab can be found in the genealogical line of Jesus.

» Instead of building monuments, the people put piles of stones to mark the location to remember what God did for them.

» The ruins of Jericho have been found by archaeologists. They are the oldest biblical ruins discovered in Israel. The city really existed!

» Moses was recorded writing down the law, and later Joshua read from the book of the law. These were all early signs of the Bible coming together.

Spies in Jericho (JOSHUA 1-4)

Joshua stepped up as the new leader of the Israelites. God promised to give them all the land as long as they kept their focus on the law—reading it, talking about it, meditating on it. If so, they will succeed. Over and over, God told Joshua, "Be strong and courageous."

The people agreed and promised their loyalty to Joshua.

> A disreputable woman like Rahab is in the family line of Jesus. She would be an ancestor of King David and Solomon. Jesus came to earth to save all people, no matter what sins they committed.

Jericho was a heavily fortified city on the other side of the Jordan River, their first stop into the Promised Land. Joshua sent two spies over to check it out. The people in the city discovered the spies were there and a manhunt was underway.

The spies encountered a woman named Rahab, a prostitute, who hid them under stalks of flax on her roof. Rahab said that the people in Jericho heard all about the Israelites' great conquests, and they were scared. She knew that God would take this city and asked if she and her family could be spared. They told her to put a red piece of rope outside her window to mark their location when the invasion began.

Returning to Joshua on the other side of the Jordan, the spies gave their report and were confident God would give them victory.

They set out for Jericho, but the huge army of 40,000 needed to cross a deep river—the Jordan. God had a plan. The Levites carried the ark of the covenant into the river first. As soon as they did, the Jordan River stopped flowing! Just like with the Red Sea, the army crossed safely to the other side while the ark and the priests held their position. Once they stepped out, the river flowed again. An incredible miracle! They marked this spot with twelve stones, one from every tribe, as a reminder of what happened.

The Wall's Fall (JOSHUA 5-6)

Other nations heard what happened at the Jordan and their hearts sank in fear.

Now the army approached Jericho and the huge walls around the city. It looked impossible to take down the city, but God had another plan. They wouldn't be fighting alone.

Joshua saw a man with a sword in his hand.

"Are you for us or against us?" Joshua asked.

"Neither," said the man. "I am commander of the Lord's army." An angel!

Joshua fell to his knees. "What should we do next?"

The Lord communicated a plan to defeat the city in seven days. First, the army must march around the city once a day for six days. The priests would carry the ark of the covenant with them while seven priests carried trumpets of ram's horns.

The seventh day was different. This time, they marched around the city seven times, and on the seventh time, the horns blasted and their voices shouted. Right then the huge walls that surrounded Jericho collapsed and the army ran right in!

They spared only Rahab and her family, who marked their window with a red piece of rope. They burned down the city and took the silver and gold, putting it into the Lord's treasury. Nothing was to be kept for anyone personally. That was a direct order from God.

Sin in the Camp (JOSHUA 7-8)

Unknown to everyone except God, a man named Achan took some items from Jericho and hid them under his tent. When it came time to defeat their next enemy, Ai, the Israelites were so confident from their victory over Jericho that they decided to send only a few thousand. They got whooped!

Joshua cried to God, "Why did this happen?" God said that someone sinned in their camp and kept some precious items from Jericho for himself. The Lord guided Joshua, family by family, until it was all narrowed down to Achan.

Joshua called out to him, "Achan, why have you done this thing?"

Achan cried, "I saw this beautiful robe and all these coins. I just had to have them!"

The items were turned over and Achan and his family received their sentence . . . death by stoning. The Israelites could not allow anyone to sin for their own selfish reasons at such a critical time in their history.

The Israelite army returned to Ai and this time won easily. Joshua built an altar to praise the Lord. He read aloud the words of the law to every Israelite.

The Longest Day (JOSHUA 9-12)

God made it very clear that the Israelites could not make a treaty with any of the enemies who lived in this territory. This was God's land, and only his people were going to live on it.

The local people of Gibeon came up with a sneaky plan. They pretended to travel from a long distance away. They made their clothes look dirty and their shoes worn. They packed their bags with dry and moldy food. As they approached the Israelites, they said they were from a far-away land and asked if they could make a treaty. After inspecting all their things, the Israelites agreed, signing a treaty to let them live.

God wasn't happy and revealed the trick to them. "Why didn't you ask me first? These are the Gibeonites, who live in the land!"

The Israelites learned their lesson—ask God first before doing anything. They let the Gibeonites live but made them their slaves.

Other kings were not so cunning and tried to attack the Israelites. A number of kings got together and formed a super-army, then marched up to Joshua and his army. But God told the Israelites not to be afraid. "I have already given them into your hands."

The battle was swift and powerful. God even threw large hailstones down on the newly created army, killing many of the enemy. Joshua then prayed that the sun would stand still while they took revenge on their enemies. God listened and delayed the sun from going down for a full day. Never had there been anything like it, when God listened to a person!

The kings that banded together were killed, followed by all the cities in the southern part of Israel. Joshua and the Israelite army were on a roll. They left no survivors, taking down everything easily, just as God asked them to.

Then Joshua and his armies moved north, taking out the armies up there. Nobody could stop them. Victory after victory. In all, thirty-one kings lost to the Israelites.

Dividing It Up (JOSHUA 13–24)

Now Joshua was very old, and it was time to divide up all the land amongst the tribes so they could settle and make it their homes. The Reubenites, Gadites, and the tribe of Manasseh returned to their land on the other side of the Jordan. The Levites, of course, had no land, since their job was to focus on the temple, but they did get certain cities all over Israel where they could live.

Joshua and Caleb, because of their faith during the spy incident over forty years ago, got their own allotment of land. Caleb, at eighty-five years old, took a portion of land known as Hebron, fighting the Anakites (big men) and driving them out. He was a tough old guy!

All the other tribes got portions of the land in Israel, but some did not completely drive out all of the enemies. This would prove to be a problem later on. One problem area was the city controlled by the Jebusites in the area Judah received. The city they could not conquer was named Jerusalem.

But for now, there was peace as everyone finally settled in the land God promised them while their ancestors lived in Egypt.

Joshua, like Moses before him, gave a farewell speech to the people. He called on the people to be strong and courageous, to love the Lord their God, to follow all the rules and remember God's promises. He emphasized clearly to fear the Lord and serve him. Joshua told all the leaders to make up their minds, once and for all, whether they should follow God or not. No more sitting on the fence.

Joshua said, "As for me and my house, we will serve the Lord!"

Joshua died at 110 years old. He was one of the last ones who remembered Egypt and lived through the wilderness experience. He was buried in Israel, as well as Joseph, whose bones had been brought up from Egypt, according to his dying wish.

Everyone settled in their places, but they needed one thing: a leader like Moses or Joshua. Without one, the people quickly forgot about God.

WHAT'S THE POINT?

▶ You can only be strong and courageous when you know God is directing you and he's on your side.

▶ Don't try to hide your sin. You could be hurting other people without knowing it.

▶ Your sinfulness doesn't disqualify you from being used by God.

▶ You will have to decide one day whether your house will serve the Lord.

7

Heroes (and Losers)

JUDGES; RUTH

WHO'S WHO

» **Ehud**—left-handed people's favorite Bible character

» **Deborah**—the only woman judge

» **Gideon**—a brave warrior who didn't know he was a brave warrior

» **Jephthah**—a man who spoke too soon

» **Samson**—the strongest man in the Bible, who got his strength from his hair

» **Ruth**—a Gentile who was the great-grandmother of King David and in the line of Christ

WHERE ARE WE?

» **Israel**—kind of like the Wild West during this time

INTERESTING STUFF IN THIS SECTION

» A judge in this book did not sit in a court with a gavel and scream "order in the court!" A judge was someone who brought "judgment" on someone, like a commander of an army taking down an enemy. However, judges weren't just military commanders. They were expected to be spiritual examples and leaders. All the judges were failures except for Deborah and Samuel.

» The book of Judges covers around four hundred years. That's more time than the United States has been around!

The Cycle (JUDGES 1–2)

After Joshua, there was no leader called to lead the nation. Instead, judges were appointed to lead each tribe. This meant that instead of working together, the tribes tried to go it alone. This was a disaster. Without allegiance to one another, the tribes continuously went through cycles of rebellion against God, oppression by other nations, deliverance by a judge, and a period of rest. It was obvious that the tribes needed a leader who could unify them into one nation; near the end of this period, the tribes were desperately looking for a king.

On top of that, the generation who served under Joshua and knew the Lord died off and was replaced by another generation who didn't know the Lord as well. Their fathers didn't do a good job inspiring them to be followers of

God, and people began serving false gods and worshiping idols, such as Baal and Ashtoreth.

History began to fall into predictable cycles. First, the enemies would rise up and oppress the people. Then the people cried out to God. God stepped in and saved them, sending a judge to defeat the enemy. The people praised God, loving him! But as time went on and the judge died, they forgot about God and returned to their sins. That's when another enemy rose up and the cycle repeated.

God was angry because after all he did for these people, they treated him like this. To teach them a lesson, he allowed their enemies to grow more powerful.

Othniel, Ehud, Shamgar (JUDGES 3)

Othniel was the first judge who volunteered to attack and capture Kiriath Sepher. He was Caleb's nephew. Othniel was successful. Other tribes, such as Benjamin, struggled to move the Jebusites out of Jerusalem. The enemies still had a foothold in different parts of Israel.

After Othniel, the people returned to evil, so God allowed Eglon, the king of the Moabites, to rise to power, attacking Israel and taking Jericho. Eglon ruled over Israel for eighteen years. The people cried out to God for help.

God raised a warrior named Ehud to power. What was unique about him? He was a left-handed person. Why was that a big deal? If a man was frisked for weapons, he was checked only on the inside left thigh, because most people were right-handed. But when left-handed Ehud asked to meet with King Eglon to give him a gift, he snuck

89

a double-edged sword into the meeting on his inside right thigh.

One night, Ehud found the king and said, "I have a secret to tell you."

King Eglon took Ehud to his private room and said, "What's the secret?"

Ehud said, "This!" He pulled out the sword with his left hand and rammed it into Eglon's stomach. His guts spilled out! Ehud snuck out. Eglon's servants knocked on the door, thinking the king was in the bathroom. When he didn't come out, they busted in and found him dead.

Meanwhile, Ehud called the army to attack, and the Moabites fell. Because of Ehud, there was peace for eighty years.

The third judge was a bit of a mystery. His name was Shamgar, and he struck down six hundred Philistines with an ox goad. An ox goad is a stick used to prod an ox and make him go. Shamgar killed hundreds with a pointy stick!

Women Power (JUDGES 4–5)

After some time passed and the Israelites returned to doing evil in God's eyes, the Lord allowed King Jabin of the Canaanites to rule over them. His army had nine hundred iron chariots, and they took over Israel for twenty years. Sisera was the feared commander of their army.

Deborah, a godly and courageous woman, led Israel when they were oppressed by the Canaanites. She was both a judge and prophetess. Hearing directly from God, she sent for Barak, the commander of the Israelite army.

"God said to take ten thousand men and go up against Sisera. You will win."

Barak hesitated. "Okay, but only if you go with us."

"Sure, I'll go, but since you hesitated, the honor of defeating Sisera will go to a woman."

Meanwhile, a man named Heber set up his tent with his wife, Jael, near Kadesh.

Nearby, Sisera prepared his armies and his chariots.

Deborah gave the go-ahead, and Barak attacked Sisera with such a crushing blow, Sisera jumped off his chariot and ran for his life. Out of breath, he found a tent near Kadesh, owned by Heber.

Sisera fell to the ground and asked for water. Heber's wife, Jael, offered him milk and asked him to come inside the tent. "Don't be afraid," Jael told him. She covered him while he lay on the ground.

Once he went to sleep, Jael took a hammer and a tent peg and rammed it into his skull. A woman defeated the great military leader just as Deborah said!

Deborah heard the news and recorded a great song with Barak. The song gave God all the praise. The land was peaceful for forty years.

Gideon the Great (JUDGES 6-9)

Wouldn't you know it, as those forty years passed, the Israelites slipped right back into their sinfulness. God decided to allow the Midianites to take over. Things got so bad, the Israelites hid in caves and mountains because the Midianites ran through and took whatever they could get their hands on. Nobody could hold on to anything because the Midianites rode in on their camels like thousands of locusts and stripped the people bare.

One night, a farmer named Gideon was working when an angel showed up and said, "The Lord is with you, mighty warrior!"

Gideon looked around, wondering whom this angel was talking to. "You talkin' to me?"

The angel told Gideon he was chosen to defeat the Midianites. Gideon doubted this was all true, so he asked for a sign. But first he prepared an offering for the Lord—a goat and bread.

The angel told Gideon to place the offering down on a rock, then *ZAP*, fire flamed up from the rock and consumed the food. The angel disappeared.

Gideon was like, "Yeah, that was definitely the Lord."

That night, the Lord told Gideon to tear down his father's altar to Baal and his Asherah pole and build a proper altar to God.

Gideon did so at night. In the morning, when everyone woke up, they saw what happened and realized Gideon did it. They were furious. They wanted to punish him and came to Gideon's father's house. His father came out and said to them, "Hey, if Baal's so tough, let him defend himself." The people walked away.

A super-army of Midianites, Amalekites, and other nations began to form to devastate Israel. The Spirit of the Lord called Gideon to battle, but Gideon wanted to make sure that he was the right person and this was the right time.

"If it's me you want to save Israel, then I'm going to lay out a fleece, and in the morning if the fleece is wet but the ground around it is dry, then I'll know what to do." He laid out the fleece and it happened as Gideon asked.

But Gideon wanted to really, really make sure. His second request exposed a lack of faith. He should have trusted God the first time. "This time I'll lay out the fleece, and in the morning if the fleece is dry and the ground wet,

then I'll know what to do." The next morning it happened just as he asked.

With everything confirmed, he gathered his forces —32,000 strong.

God told Gideon, "That's too many men. People will think your numbers won the war and not me. So tell the army if anyone's scared, they can go home." Gideon did, and 22,000 took off. Ten thousand were left.

God didn't like the numbers. "Too many. Separate the ones who drink water with a cupped hand from those who lap the water like a dog." Gideon took his army to a river and separated them again. Only three hundred drank with a cupped hand. God was pleased.

Gideon handed out trumpets, jars, and torches (not bows, arrows, and spears). "Follow me," he said, and the army snuck into the Midianite camp at night.

Everyone put their torches in the jars, and when they received the signal, everyone blew their trumpets and smashed the jars, revealing the torches. This startled the

Midianite army, and they began to stab each other with their swords in confusion. Gideon was indeed a mighty warrior.

Gideon kept peace there in Israel for forty years, but the people returned to the Baals, the same altars Gideon tore down.

Abimelek, Gideon's son, tried to take over for him, but he was kind of a loser. A woman dropped a millstone on his head, killing him, so that really didn't go anywhere.

Six More Judges (JUDGES 10-12)

Some of the judges God appointed have incredible stories. Others we know very little about. For example, Tola ruled for twenty-three years and Jair ruled for twenty-two years. Whatever they did and however they did it, they were effective.

As always, the Israelites returned to their evil ways, serving meaningless gods from other nations. They finally found themselves slaves to other nations, not just slaves to their gods. God heard their cry and responded again by raising up an unlikely hero.

Jephthah's brothers didn't like him because he was the son of a prostitute, so they kicked him out. After he was kicked out, he organized a band of outlaws. Then, as the tribe struggled to find a leader to fight the Ammonites, they realized Jephthah was the best.

"Would you be our commander?" they asked Jephthah.

"Really? Are you going to kick me out again once I win?" he replied.

"No, we will do whatever you say!"

Jephthah agreed and led the army. He sent a message to the Ammonites, warning them that God was on their side. They didn't care.

The Spirit of the Lord filled Jephthah. He could feel the power, but he made a hasty promise. "God, if you help us win, I will sacrifice the first thing that comes out the door of my house to greet me!" That wasn't very smart.

Jephthah and his army devastated twenty towns and beat the Ammonites.

Then he returned home, and his daughter was the first one to run out of the house to greet him. Jephthah remembered his promise. He was sad. His daughter was brave and didn't want her daddy to be disgraced before God. She celebrated his victory and allowed him to follow through to honor God. She is an example of another godly woman during the time of the judges.

Jephthah led for six years.

Three more judges led at different times—Ibzan, Elon, and Abdon. Some judges ruled by having many sons and daughters work together as a family, trusting each other.

God used all of them, but none was more famous, more frightening, more powerful than Samson.

The Strongest Man Ever (JUDGES 13–15)

Well, you know the story by now. The Lord got mad at the Israelites because they returned to their evil ways. This time the Philistines took over for forty years! But God had a special judge in mind this time.

There was this man named Manoah, and he and his wife could not have children. An angel showed up and told them they would have a son, but asked them to make sure this boy never drank wine, never touched anything unclean, and never cut his hair. It was all part of a Nazirite vow. She gave birth and they named the child Samson.

Samson joined the ranks of Isaac, John the Baptist, and Jesus of having their births announced by an angel.

Samson grew up and "fell in love" with a woman who was a Philistine. His parents didn't like his choice in women, but God was using this for Samson's defeat of the Philistines. Samson married the girl.

The Spirit of the Lord came upon him and he was strong. One time, he tore a lion in half. Another time, he made a bet that nobody could figure out his riddle, and when they did, he stripped the clothes off the backs of one group and gave them to another.

Samson's father-in-law gave Samson's wife away to another man when he didn't think Samson loved her anymore. Samson flipped out. He caught three hundred foxes, tied them together in twos with a torch between them, and set them loose in the Philistine fields. All their crops burned up.

> Gaza to Hebron is thirty-seven miles. The gates of the city weigh at least a ton—total or each.

When the Philistines came to apprehend Samson, he broke out of the ropes and killed a thousand men with the jawbone of a donkey. He violated his Nazirite vow by touching something that was dead and unclean. A group of men in Gaza waited to capture Samson, but Samson instead tore off the gates of the city and carried them far away to Hebron.

Samson's Hair-Raising Secret (JUDGES 16)

The Philistines offered a reward for Samson's capture; they asked his girlfriend, Delilah, to help them.

Delilah asked Samson to tell her the secret to his strength. Over and over she begged, until Samson started telling lies just to have some fun. But after several lies and several attempts by the Philistines to capture him, Samson finally told Delilah the truth: "If you cut my hair, I will lose my strength!"

So she did! Once Samson's hair was cut, his strength disappeared, and the Philistines overpowered him. They removed his eyes and made him grind grain.

Pleased with their conquest of Samson, the Philistines decided to bring him into a stadium to make fun of him. But what they didn't know was that Samson's hair was growing back and his strength was returning.

Samson entered the stadium and talked to a little boy, asking him to put his hands on the pillars that held up the building. He prayed for God's strength and pushed as hard as he could!

The stadium came crashing down, killing Samson and thousands of Philistines. This final act quieted the

Philistines and brought peace to Israel. Samson had judged Israel for twenty years.

Not a Happy Ending (JUDGES 17–21)

Israel continued to spin out of control. God did not raise up any more judges after Samson. The people could not learn their lesson. Tribe began to fight against tribe. Brother against brother. The people worshiped idols and began to commit crimes without any guilt.

Things got so bad, a woman was attacked by a group of men in the town of Gibeah. When all the other tribes found out about it, they punished Gibeah and the tribe of Benjamin.

Then everyone felt bad for hurting the tribe of Benjamin, and one mistake after another was made. The tribes were divided.

The problem: In those days, there was no king and everyone did whatever they wanted to, never once asking God for advice.

God began to fix all that.

Ruth's Baby (RUTH)

During this time of the judges, a famine struck, and a man named Elimelek from Bethlehem took his wife, Naomi, and two sons to Moab, where the famine was not so bad. They lived there a long time, until his sons married two Moabites, whose names were Orpah and Ruth.

Sadly, Elimelek and his two sons died, leaving Naomi as a widow, so she decided to return home to Bethlehem. She told her two daughters-in-law they could go back to Moab; they didn't have to stick around.

Orpah kissed Ruth good-bye, but Ruth wanted to stay. "Your home is my home," Ruth declared. Naomi took her to Bethlehem. Things would be tough for these two widows all by themselves.

Ruth went out to pick grain from a field owned by Naomi's distant relative, Boaz, who was from the line of Judah. Boaz took kindly to Ruth and made sure she was protected while picking. He had heard of her, since it was unusual for someone to stay by their mother-in-law's side once their husband died. Because of that, Boaz did nice things for Ruth.

Naomi saw an opportunity for Ruth to marry Boaz and make her part of the family again. Naomi gave Ruth some dating advice, which Ruth did, and now that Boaz knew Ruth was interested in him, he pursued her.

Once they took care of some legal arrangements, Boaz married Ruth. The whole town was impressed by Ruth's devotion to Naomi and to the Israelites.

> All of these people are in Jesus' genealogy. Though they didn't know it at the time, they would be very important in bringing a savior to the world!

Ruth and Boaz had a son named Obed. Later on, Obed married and had a number of sons, one of them named Jesse, who later also had sons. One of them was a boy named David. Ruth was David's great-grandmother, and he would become the future king of Israel.

God was working to bring about a solution to Israel's sin problem.

WHAT'S THE POINT?

▸ We also fall into cycles of loving God, ignoring him, getting in trouble, then asking for his help and returning to him.

▸ Our strength is not in our hair, muscles, looks, or skills. Our strength is in our relationship with God.

▸ Our job is not to judge, but God may use us to show people he's not happy with them.

▸ God will use you uniquely to complete his plan.

8

A Kingdom Comes
1 SAMUEL; 1 CHRONICLES 10

 WHO'S WHO

» **Hannah**—Samuel's sweet momma

» **Samuel**—the last judge (and also a prophet like Deborah) who God had his hand on since he was a little boy

» **Saul**—tall, good-looking people don't always make the best kings

» **David**—a superstar shepherd and expert stone-thrower

» **Goliath**—the bigger they are, the harder they fall

 WHERE ARE WE?

» **Shiloh**—currently where the ark of the covenant is parked

» **Bethlehem**—David's hometown

» **Gath**—Goliath's hometown

INTERESTING STUFF IN THIS SECTION

» God planned to give Israel a king, but not like other nations. The king in Israel was supposed to rule as a servant who trusted in God—not in his army, and not becoming greedy for money and power. He was to be totally different from the kings of pagan nations.

» First and 2 Samuel were one scroll, but it was so big that the Bible compilers made it two books.

» Anointing someone with oil was simply an act of pouring oil on someone's head. It was meant to show God's favor or approval as the person's life was covered by God.

» An armor-bearer acted like a caddy for a golfer. They carried necessary weapons for the soldier, but they could also jump into the fight if needed.

» Samuel is one of only two books that mention cheese (the other is Job).

» Goliath's height was somewhere between seven feet and nine feet tall. He was big, but he was slow.

Sam the Man (1 SAMUEL 1-3)

A man named Elkanah had a sweet wife named Hannah who didn't have any children. She prayed constantly that she could have a child.

Meanwhile, the ark was sitting in a place called Shiloh, a temporary rest stop. Two priests ran the place—Hophni and Phineas, sons of Eli. They were evil and taking the best sacrifices for themselves to eat.

Hannah visited Shiloh to pray and, in her deep sadness, began crying, her body shaking violently. Eli watched her. It was unusual to see someone so passionate about the Lord. Eli blessed her and she went home.

Later, Hannah and her husband had a baby! Hannah was thrilled and named her son Samuel, which means "God heard." After dedicating the baby according to the Jewish rules, Hannah decided that when Samuel reached three years old, she would give the baby to the Lord, literally. Hannah dropped the boy off at Shiloh to work with Eli.

Hophni and Phineas were hated by the locals and by God. Samuel, though, was a good boy. Hannah made him a little priest's outfit and for years he served faithfully, better than Eli's sons.

A man showed up and gave a prophecy. He said Eli's sons would die on the same day and God would raise up a proper priest. This was unusual because God wasn't really speaking to people on a regular basis.

One night, little Samuel tried to sleep, but a voice called him: "Samuel!" Samuel walked into Eli's room and asked what he wanted. Eli had not called him. This happened two more times until Eli figured out what was going on. God was calling the boy. Eli said, "When you hear the voice, say, 'Speak, your servant is listening.'"

Samuel heard the voice and said what Eli told him to say. The Lord answered, "I'm about to do something amazing in Israel. I will also carry out a punishment against Eli for how he and his sons have treated my house."

Eli called Samuel in and asked what the Lord said. Samuel didn't lie.

Eli understood when he heard the news. "He's the Lord, let him do what he wants to do."

The Ark Is Gone! (1 SAMUEL 4–7)

The Israelites tried to fight the Philistines, but they couldn't hold them back. Then the Israelites had an idea: They wanted to take the ark into battle to see if that would help them win. It didn't. In fact, the Philistines captured the ark and took it with them.

Eli's two sons died when the ark was taken. Someone ran to town and told Eli the news. When he heard that his sons were dead, Eli, who was old and very fat, fell backwards off his chair and broke his neck. The whole family line was wiped out in one day.

Now that the Philistines had the ark, strange things started to happen to them. They put the ark in the temple to their gods, but in the morning, their idols were lying face-first before the ark, the head and hands broken off. Then people started to get tumors. They understood why—it was that ark!

They returned the ark to the Israelites on a cart pulled by two cows. Also included were golden gifts to this God who had so much power. Some people looked inside the ark or touched it and were killed. Everybody forgot to treat this ark with respect.

The Israelites rejoiced when the ark returned. They put it in the house of a man named Abinadab. His whole house prospered while the ark was there.

Samuel, now a priest and a leader of Israel, told the nation to return to God and commit their ways to him. They agreed and began to defeat the Philistines every chance they got.

Who Wants to Be King? (1 SAMUEL 8–15)

Later on, there were no good leaders amongst the Israelites, and Samuel was getting old. The Israelites looked at other nations and saw they had kings, so they said, "We want a king, too."

Samuel told them that kings lose control, get greedy, and make life difficult if you give them so much power. Kings are just people; they have faults, too. They tax heavily and steal your daughters. Still, the people said, "Whatever, we still want a king!"

There was this guy named Saul, from the tribe of Benjamin. He was tall and good-looking. His father's donkeys were lost and Saul went looking for them. Saul's servant had mentioned that there was a prophet who lived nearby. Maybe he could tell them where the donkeys were.

Meanwhile, God spoke to Samuel and said, "There's a guy coming to see you and he's going to be king of Israel." Samuel was ready. When Saul arrived, they talked about the great things God was going to do through Saul. (And, yes, the donkeys were found.)

The Spirit of God entered Saul and he began to prophesy. Samuel assembled all the heads of the tribes for a vote. Saul was chosen as king, but he had gone into hiding, as he was afraid. They brought him out and the people shouted, "Long live the king!"

Saul proved himself worthy to be king by leading an army to save a place called Jabesh Gilead, held captive by the Ammonites. When he won the conflict, the people confirmed him as king.

Now there was a new kind of leader in place, a king— not a prophet, judge, or priest—so Samuel stepped aside. He warned them about the problems of a king, then said it really came down to them keeping the Lord's commands. Saul prayed for the nation.

Later, Saul prepared to fight against the Philistines with his son Jonathan. Samuel said to wait for him and, as a priest, he would offer a sacrifice to God. When Samuel didn't show up, Saul did the sacrifice himself—something only a priest should do. Samuel arrived and saw what Saul had done. He said, "Your kingdom will fail. God has found a man after his own heart."

Led mostly by Jonathan, the Israelites won victories against the Philistine armies. Things between father and son grew cold, with many disagreements. Saul didn't listen to God. One time, God told Saul to kill everything in sight when he attacked Agag, king of the Amalekites. Saul spared the sheep. When Samuel caught him, he confirmed that Saul would lose his kingdom.

Saul knew he had sinned. Samuel never visited him again.

It was time for a new king. Enter the greatest king Israel ever had.

David, the Giant-Killer (1 SAMUEL 16–17)

God told Samuel to go to Bethlehem. There, Samuel would find God's chosen king. When Samuel arrived, God told him not to judge the king by his appearance or height, because God doesn't choose people the way people choose people. God said, "I look at the heart."

A man named Jesse had seven sons, and Samuel asked to see them all. One by one, they walked past Samuel.

None of them was the one God chose. "Is that all of your sons?" Samuel asked.

Jesse replied, "There's one more. The youngest. But he's working the fields as a shepherd today."

"Get him," Samuel said.

When David arrived, Samuel knew he was the one. Samuel anointed David with oil, and the Lord filled David's heart.

At the same time, the Spirit left Saul, leaving him open to an evil spirit who tormented him. He had outbursts of anger, but his servants felt music would help. It just so happened that David played the lyre and was hired to calm Saul. Saul liked him and promoted him to armor-bearer.

Around this time, the Philistines faced off with an Israelite army in the Valley of Elah. Their best warrior, Goliath, stepped out with a challenge. He was taller, bigger, and meaner than any pro wrestler or NBA star. His offer was this: a one-on-one battle, winner takes all. Anyone who can beat Goliath wins the war.

Nobody stepped forward. They were at a standstill. Saul even offered his daughter's hand in the deal. The winner would be the son of a king! Still nothing.

David showed up to deliver grain, cheese, and bread to his brave brothers in the army and heard about the challenge. He heard Goliath say terrible things about God. David said, "I'll fight him."

Everyone laughed. King Saul couldn't believe it. They were going to risk everything on a little shepherd boy?

David made his case. "I've killed lions and bears with my slingshot. I can take this guy out." David put aside the armor soldiers usually wear, trusting God to protect him instead. He gathered five stones in his arsenal and stepped out.

This time Goliath laughed. But David was serious. "You have all these weapons, but I come to you in the name of the Lord. I'll take you down and cut off your head."

Then David charged Goliath, loading his sling with the first and only stone he would need. The stone flew through the air and, before Goliath knew what happened, the rock imbedded in his forehead, killing him on contact. David pulled out his sword and cut off Goliath's head, just as he said he would. The crowd went wild and the Israelites chased the Philistines away. David became a huge hero, bigger than Saul ever was.

A Jealous King (1 SAMUEL 18-24)

Saul didn't like that the people loved David more than him. They shouted that Saul might have killed thousands, but David killed tens of thousands. Even Saul's son Jonathan loved David. This jealousy completely overran Saul, throwing him into fits of rage that David tried to calm with music. Saul only threw spears at him.

David was offered Saul's daughter Michal in marriage. David went out and killed two hundred more Philistines in payment for her hand.

The family dynamics got very awkward. David was the son-in-law of King Saul, but Saul told his son Jonathan— also best friend to David—to kill David. David ran and hid throughout the country.

During this time, David and Jonathan grew closer, meeting secretly. When Saul figured Jonathan liked David more than him, he tried to kill Jonathan.

David gathered an army of expert fighting men, who battled Israel's enemies and protected the man they believed should be king. Along the way, David made friends with prophets and priests, but some died by Saul's orders because of their allegiance to David.

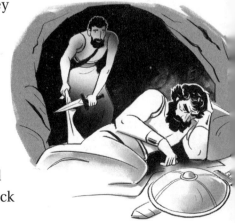

One time, while Saul slept in a cave, David snuck

up close enough to kill Saul, but didn't, only taking a piece of his clothing. Once a safe distance away, David cried out, "Look, I have proof I was right next to you while you slept, but I didn't kill you." Saul would repent of his anger but later turn around and give orders to kill David again. Saul was a mess.

Saul Falls (1 SAMUEL 25–31; 1 CHRONICLES 10)

Samuel eventually died, leaving a huge leadership hole in Israel, especially with Saul losing his mind.

David continued to roam around Israel, running from Saul. He saved a nice woman named Abigail from her mean husband and ended up marrying her when her husband died.

Saul heard where David was hiding and went out after him. Just like the time in the cave, David snuck into Saul's camp, took Saul's spear and water jug, then woke everyone once he was a safe distance away. "You have terrible security, Saul. Look what I took. But I didn't kill you. Don't you see my loyalty?" Saul did and called David a blessed man for being so loyal despite Saul's attacks.

David had an interesting tactic to protect himself against Saul. He lived with the enemy, the Philistines. Saul would never hunt him down across enemy lines. The Philistines were scared of David—remember, he killed Goliath.

Saul needed advice, and he had heard of a woman in Endor who spoke to the dead. Saul had outlawed all mediums, or dead-talkers, but he needed one right now. He

wanted advice from the long-departed Samuel. The me-
dium reluctantly tried to make contact, but God allowed
it to happen. Samuel's spirit spoke to Saul and he didn't
have nice things to say.

"Why are you bothering me?" Samuel said. "God is taking your kingdom away from you, and tomorrow you and
your sons will die!" Saul lay on the ground, processing the
terrible news—in twenty-four hours he would be dead.

The Philistines were on a rampage, and so were the
Amalekites. While David and his army were fighting the
Philistines, the Amalekites swarmed into David's home
base, Ziklag. They burned it and took all the women and
children, including David's wives.

David and a small army defeated the Amalekites, safely
rescuing everyone's families.

The Philistines were after Saul and they killed all of his
sons, including Jonathan, David's best friend. An archer
fired an arrow that critically wounded him.

Saul didn't want to be turned over alive to his enemies (a dishonorable surrender for a soldier), so he asked his armor-bearer to kill him. The armor-bearer could not do it, so Saul picked himself up and fell on his sword. The prophecy from Samuel came true—Saul and his sons were dead.

The Philistines cut off Saul's head and stripped him of his armor. They put it all on display at their god's temple, giving their false god credit for the victory. A group of Israelites from Jabesh Gilead took the bodies of Saul and his sons and gave them a proper burial.

The reign of Saul was over. The reign of David was about to begin.

WHAT'S THE POINT?

- ▶ Be careful who you make your boss. God must be the first one you listen to.

- ▶ Faith defeats giants. If God is on your side, no one can beat you.

- ▶ God chooses the most unlikely people to lead.

- ▶ Don't try to be the boss; let God establish you as the boss.

9

The Greatest Kings

2 SAMUEL; 1 KINGS 1–11; 1 AND 2 CHRONICLES

WHO'S WHO

» **David**—one of the greatest kings of all time, but certainly not perfect
» **Bathsheba**—needs to be careful where she takes a bath
» **Nathan**—a prophet who had to tell a king he was wrong
» **Solomon**—a really wise guy

WHERE ARE WE?

» **Jerusalem**—officially the current-day capital of Israel

INTERESTING STUFF IN THIS SECTION

» David captures Jerusalem and makes it the capital of Israel.

» David's first ten sons include (in order): Amnon, Daniel, Absalom, Adonijah, Shephatiah, Ithream, Shammua, Shobab, Nathan, Solomon.

» David's mighty warriors included Jashobeam, Eleazar, Abishai, Amasai, Benaiah, and others. A total of thirty achieved that status in David's army.

» The Gadite warriors were said to have the faces of lions and the swiftness of gazelles.

» David had administrators in charge of camels, donkeys, and even olive oil.

» Solomon was originally named Jedidiah.

Long Live the King! (2 SAMUEL 1–5; 1 CHRONICLES 11:1–9, 14)

While David fought against the Amalekites, a man stumbled in to give David the news.

"Saul and his son Jonathan are dead."

David tore his clothes in anguish. His king and best friend were dead. David, a songwriter, wrote a sad song to explain his grief.

Once the time of mourning was over, David went to a town named Hebron, where the residents anointed him as king. He was king of Hebron for seven years and six months.

During that period, small squabbles broke out between soldiers loyal to Saul and those loyal to David. The fighting got many killed. Most of Saul's family was killed. Only

Mephibosheth, son of Jonathan, survived. But he was dropped during an escape and both of his feet became disabled.

As the battles came to an end, all the tribes of Israel came to an agreement—David was their next king! He was thirty years old at the time.

The Jebusites lived in Jerusalem, a city high up on a hill. David managed to conquer them and took over the fortress. He liked the city; it became known as the City of David. He lived in the fortress with his whole family while construction began on his actual palace. Jerusalem became the capital of Israel. All the while, David won victory after victory, beating the Philistines.

A New Day (2 SAMUEL 6-10; 1 CHRONICLES 13-19)

Finally, the ark of the covenant—the ark that Moses and the Israelites carried through the wilderness for forty years, that marched around Jericho, that was carried into battle after battle—finally made its way to Jerusalem, its permanent location.

It was a massive celebration with David, the king, leaping and dancing in the streets. Everyone in the city was treated to bread and cakes. David danced so wildly, his wife Michal was embarrassed. David didn't care. The ark was finally in Jerusalem; however, it was parked in a simple tent.

Then God spoke to David, making a promise that would forever change the world. It began with David wanting to build a temple for God, to make God's name great. God appreciated the thought but said David's son would build it. David killed too many people and the temple was about peace and reconciliation.

God then promised, "Your house and your kingdom will endure forever before me, your throne will be established forever." David prayed and praised God for his power.

That promise pointed right to Jesus, who would be in the family line of David, down to Mary and Joseph. Only Jesus could reign as king forever.

David found favor with God, with victory after victory against enemies. He built a loyal and powerful army and appointed impressive officials to run all matters in the kingdom.

Deep in his heart, David wanted to honor Jonathan and asked if there was anyone in his family who was still alive. A servant of Saul's household was called in, Ziba, who knew of only Jonathan's son—Mephibosheth, the one who couldn't walk. David called for him.

Thereafter, David invited Mephibosheth to dine at his table every night. It was a beautiful story of someone overlooked by many but recognized and loved by the king.

David Sins Big-Time (2 SAMUEL 11-12; 1 CHRONICLES 20:1-3)

David should have been at war, fighting as kings do, but he decided to stay home. One night, he looked out from his bed and saw a beautiful woman bathing on her rooftop. He told her servants to bring her to him.

This wasn't his wife. David committed adultery.

When the woman, named Bathsheba, later told David that she was pregnant, he tried to cover it up. When her husband, Uriah, refused to cooperate with David, David had him set up to be killed on the battlefield.

Now David had committed murder.

After Bathsheba mourned her husband, she moved into the palace and married David.

A prophet named Nathan came up to the king and, risking his life, told David a story: "A rich man had a whole bunch of sheep, but he saw a poor man with a little lamb, his only one. The rich man took the poor man's little lamb and ate it."

David was angry hearing that story, especially as a former shepherd. "What kind of person would do such a thing!"

"You, David. You are that person. You took Uriah's wife and killed him for her."

David hung his head. "Yes, yes, I did. I have sinned against God."

"Your family will suffer many consequences. In fact, the baby she's carrying will die." Nathan was right. The baby was born but died soon afterward.

Bathsheba did have another child. His name was Solomon. More on him later.

Family Feuds (2 SAMUEL 13-19)

David's family did experience lots of problems, especially with his children born to different mothers. One in particular, Absalom, was a handsome man, with thick, flowing hair. So thick, it weighed five pounds when they cut it. He wanted to be king after his father, and even influenced people to think he should be king.

The support for Absalom grew, but David could not kill his own son! So David ran away. He encountered betrayal and attacks, people shaming him for his actions. But God took care of the situation.

One day, David's troops spotted Absalom's men and a battle broke out. Absalom took off on his horse, but his long, beautiful, thick hair got caught in a tree. He hung from a branch by his hair! David's men found him, but only one was brave enough to kill Absalom.

David heard the news and mourned. He returned to Jerusalem, feeling his family splinter and shatter.

David's Final Stretch (1 SAMUEL 20-1 KINGS 1; 1 CHRONICLES 20-21)

David's time as king ended without all the parades and cheers as when he started. Politically, he kept promises. Militarily, they won wars. The whole time David sang praises to his God.

His mighty warriors fought incredible battles. Goliath's brother was killed, as well as a huge man with six fingers on each hand and six toes on each foot. One of his warriors killed eight hundred men in one encounter, another killed three hundred. Another fought a lion in a pit on a snowy day. And yet another fought a battle so hard his hand froze to the sword. They would do anything for their king—even kill to get him a cup of water.

David failed to be the man of God he once was. One time, he had his commander count his army. When he returned with the number—800,000—David felt bad. He counted the army for selfish reasons, not godly reasons.

A prophet named Gad spoke to the king about this. "You've angered the Lord and he's offered to punish you in one of three ways—three years of famine, three months of enemy attack, or three days of plague? Which do you prefer?"

David saw how bad each of them was. He didn't want to choose. So God chose for him. Three days of plague. Seventy thousand died.

David cried out when he saw an angel. "Enough! I can't take it! I have sinned! I'm the shepherd! These people are just sheep! Punish me!" The angel stopped the plague.

Gad told David to go back to that place where he saw the angel and build an altar. David purchased the location—a threshing floor to process wheat—and built an altar.

That place was on Mount Moriah. It will be where David's son Solomon will soon build the temple.

David grew very old, and the question of which son would be the next king came up. David very firmly said, "Solomon." Not everyone liked that choice, especially another of David's sons, Adonijah, who tried, unsuccessfully, to make himself king.

Solomon, the Wisest Guy (1 KINGS 2-4; 1 CHRONICLES 29-2 CHRONICLES 1:12)

David took his son Solomon aside and gave him some advice. "If you're going to be king, be strong and act like a man. Focus on God's laws, walk in obedience, and you'll be successful."

David died. Solomon took over, straightening out certain matters his father had left undone. He kept his promise to his father by walking according to God's laws . . . for now.

The Lord appeared to Solomon in a dream. "Ask for whatever you want me to give you." Solomon had lots of choices—long life, wealth, power.

Instead, he said this: "I'm young and I don't know what I'm doing. Give me wisdom to govern your people, so I can know right from wrong."

God was impressed. "I will do that, and since you didn't ask for long life, wealth, and power, I'll give you those too."

Solomon's wisdom became world-renowned. He was able to make very wise decisions to difficult problems. People from all over came to ask him questions about plant life, nature, animals, birds, reptiles, fish. He wrote over three thousand proverbs and one thousand songs. He was smarter than any other person in the world.

The people of Israel were happy. No countries were at war with Solomon. Everyone had money because the economy soared. Gold and silver were as common as pavement on the sidewalk.

The Temple Is Open for Business (1 KINGS 5–8; 2 CHRONICLES 2–7:10)

Solomon's father, David, set up connections with other kings to supply the materials necessary to construct the temple. Solomon had the lumber and stones shipped in, then put over 180,000 people to work to assemble the temple. The best craftsmen made the temple beautiful.

The temple was built with the finest lumber in the land, and it was covered all over by gold. All the furnishings of the temple needed to be handcrafted. The entire construction took seven years.

Then came the big day—the ark would be placed in the temple. For the people, this completed God's plan to build a nation, and finally the ark would no longer be in a portable tent, but in its own house. God finally had a home on earth! The people sacrificed animals as an expression of praise to God. People sang, praised, and wept.

God himself appeared in a cloud at the temple, in what's called the Holy Place, where the ark was stored. He dwelled behind a thick curtain, the holiest of holy places.

Solomon prayed, thanking God, committing the nation to him, promising to keep all his commands. The temple was dedicated with more offerings and the city partied for fourteen days.

It took many people to keep the temple running. Gate-keepers were essentially guards, making sure the right people entered the temple. Musicians played instruments and a choir sang praises.

The Wise King Acts Dumb (1 KINGS 9–11; 2 CHRONICLES 7–9)

God came to Solomon and confirmed the same promise he gave to David: "I will establish your royal throne forever. You will always have a successor on the throne." But God warned him, "Don't worship other gods or all you built will become a heap of rubble."

So Solomon built a palace for himself that took fourteen years to build—seven years more than the temple. Solomon's house was nicer than God's house. His throne was covered in ivory and gold.

Solomon built up Jerusalem with more and more buildings, using people as slave labor. He built a huge fleet of ships, and had thousands of horses and tons of chariots. Solomon built a powerful empire.

Kings of other nations admired him for his wealth and wisdom. His most famous visitor was the queen of Sheba. She had heard of his fame and brought him gifts, and was amazed how the Lord had blessed Solomon.

Solomon did a dumb thing. He did not keep his promise to the Lord. He worshiped other gods in places outside the city, high up in the mountains. He married seven hundred women. Solomon's wives came from other nations and brought their gods with them. He built them altars so they could worship their gods inside Israel.

He worshiped his wives' gods, such as Ashtoreth, Chemosh, and Molek. God was very angry. David sinned, yes, but he never worshiped other gods! God promised to tear this kingdom apart when Solomon's son Rehoboam took office.

Enemies within began to get louder. Some left Israel because they were so unhappy with Solomon and how he ran the country. One of his critics, Jeroboam, rebelled against Solomon, and people started listening to him.

A prophet came to him and tore his cloak into twelve pieces. He gave ten of those pieces to Jeroboam. "God will divide this nation of twelve tribes in half. Ten tribes will follow you and two will remain loyal to Solomon's line." Solomon tried to kill Jeroboam, but he escaped to Egypt.

After forty years as king, Solomon died. His son Rehoboam took over.

Solomon's wisdom fills the book of Proverbs, and he wrote a beautiful play called "Song of Songs." However, in the book of Ecclesiastes, Solomon, in his old age, realized his stupidity and the meaningless pursuit of worldly power, objects, and wealth. He realized that worshiping the God of one's youth was the most important thing a person could do.

WHAT'S THE POINT?

▸ When you sin, many people get hurt, including your family.

▸ Wisdom is the best thing to ask for.

▸ Even smart people do dumb things.

▸ Listen to people older than you. They have lived life and were once your age.

10

The Northern Kingdom

1 KINGS; 2 KINGS; 2 CHRONICLES

WHO'S WHO

» **Jeroboam**—a rebel who split a nation

» **Elijah**—one of the greatest prophets ever

» **Elisha**—took over and became the second-greatest prophet ever

» **Ahab**—one of the worst kings ever

» **Jezebel**—one of the worst queens ever

WHERE ARE WE?

» **Samaria**—a poor substitute for Jerusalem

INTERESTING STUFF IN THIS SECTION

» The problem in this section explains why people in Jesus' time didn't like Samaritans.

» It gets confusing, but the northern nation is known as Israel, even though the whole nation was known as Israel.

» Ten tribes formed this new nation in the north, except for Judah and Benjamin, two tribes in the south.

» Elijah was from the city Tisbe in Gilead.

Civil War (1 KINGS 12-14:21; 2 CHRONICLES 10-12)

When Rehoboam took over, the people were weary after all the building projects and wanted a little break. Rehoboam consulted his father's wise friends for advice. They said to back off and let the people relax. Then he went to his own friends. They said, "Make 'em work, bro. This is no time to be weak!"

Rehoboam listened to his friends and increased the work. "My little finger is bigger than my dad's waist! Don't mess with me!" Ten nations to the north refused and broke off all relations with the two nations to the south. Jeroboam led the revolt and became their king instead. Rehoboam wanted to go to war, but his advisers said no.

They had one big problem, though. The law of Moses said all sacrifices could only occur in the temple with priests from the line of Aaron. All those priests were in the Southern Kingdom.

So Jeroboam and the tribes in the north started their own temple in the cities of Bethel and Daniel . . . and they made a bigger mistake—they worshiped golden calves.

Jeroboam approved and invited everyone to worship these false idols. He built lots of shrines in multiple high places. God was not going to bless these decisions.

Jeroboam's son Abijah became ill, so Jeroboam sent his wife, in disguise, to the blind prophet Ahijah. "Ask him what will happen to our son." She went, but God had warned Ahijah that Jeroboam's wife was coming, so the disguise didn't do any good. He called her out and said, "The minute you go home, your son will die." As soon as she went home, guess what—the prophet was right.

Lots of Dead Kings (1 KINGS 15:25–1 KINGS 16; 2 CHRONICLES 13–16)

Nadab, Jeroboam's other son, became king. He reigned for only two years.

Baasha killed Nadab and took over as king. He was king for twenty-four years.

Elah was next, and he reigned for two years. Then one of his officials, Zimri, killed him.

Zimri lasted seven days on the throne until an army commander named Omri surrounded the city and burned down Zimri's palace, killing him.

Omri was now king. He hung in there for twelve years and built a city called Samaria, up on a hill. His son took over and became one of

> Samaritans in Jesus' day were disliked because they came from Samaria, whose legacy was known for the gods they worshiped.

the most evil kings in Northern Israel history. His name was Ahab, and his wife was Jezebel.

Ahab constructed temples to gods in Samaria. God saw all that Ahab was doing and could do, and needed to send a strong prophet to stop him. This prophet was one of the greatest in the history of prophets. His name was Elijah.

Elijah Versus 450 (1 KINGS 17-18)

God sent Elijah to King Ahab to announce a drought for a few years. It wouldn't go away unless God said so.

God took care of Elijah, despite the drought. He had ravens deliver food to him, like Uber Eats, and kept water flowing from a tiny stream. Elijah stayed at a widow's house, and God multiplied flour and olive oil into jars that were miraculously filled every day.

> Jesus would revive a young girl, a young man, and an older man to life, then himself.

When the widow's son died, Elijah laid the boy on the bed and prayed for God to revive him. The boy returned to life.

Angry at God's prophets for causing this famine, Ahab's wife, Jezebel, began killing them. Obadiah, who worked in Ahab's palace, hid many prophets in caves. Elijah was the most wanted of all the prophets, but he decided to confront Ahab face-to-face.

Elijah challenged Ahab, Jezebel, and all the priests who worked for the false gods to a test. He asked for 450

prophets of Baal and four hundred prophets of Asherah to meet on Mount Carmel.

The challenge: Whoever calls on their god and he answers by lighting a fire wins. They all agreed.

But the 450 priests of Baal showed up with a huge crowd to watch the showdown. Elijah told them to sacrifice bulls, then to call on their god to light the fire to burn them. The prophets of Baal cried, danced, screamed, even cut themselves. No answer. Elijah ridiculed them, "Shout louder! Your god may be asleep!" Morning to afternoon . . . dead silence.

Elijah was so great in God's eyes, he earned a place— along with Moses— next to Jesus on the Mount of Transfiguration.

Elijah told them to step aside. He asked the people to dig a trench around the sacrifice and dump buckets of water on the dead bulls. Once, twice, three times the sacrifices were soaked. Then he called out to God, "Lord, let your name be known today. Let everyone here know you are the God of Israel!"

At that moment, fire swooped down and burned up the sacrifices, even though they were soaking wet. The crowd cheered. "The Lord . . . he is God!"

Elijah directed the people to kill the false prophets of a false god.

Off in the distance, a small cloud appeared in the sky. Rain was coming.

Run for Your Life (1 KINGS 19)

Jezebel was so upset that Elijah had all her prophets killed, she promised him he would be dead by the next day. Elijah panicked and ran.

He ended up in the wilderness and pleaded with God to take his life. After a nap, an angel woke Elijah and told him to get something to eat. Miraculously, bread was baking on a fire next to him, and there was a jar of water.

Feeling better, Elijah walked forty days and forty nights to Mount Horeb (where Moses had met God for the first time), and took a nap in a cave.

The next day, God asked him, "What are you doing here, Elijah?"

Elijah replied, "I've been very excited about you, but the Israelites aren't. They reject all your laws, have torn down your altars, and put your prophets to death. I'm the last one!"

A wind tore through the mountain, but the Lord wasn't in the wind. An earthquake rattled the mountain, but God wasn't in the mountain. A fire burned up the mountain, but God wasn't in that either.

Then there was a whisper, and God was in that. "Go back to where you came from. I want you to confirm some new leaders. I'll set aside seven thousand true believers. And go find a guy named Elisha and make him your apprentice."

As Elijah returned home, he saw Elisha plowing his field with oxen. Elijah put his cloak around Elisha, a sign to follow Elijah. Elisha burned up the plow and killed both oxen for a feast, then left his family to follow Elijah.

Ahab's Final Battles (1 KINGS 20-22:40; 2 CHRONICLES 17-21)

Ben-Hadad, king of Aram, surrounded Samaria (Ahab's capital city). God sent a prophet to tell Ahab how to win the battle. Ahab followed the instructions and won. The next spring, Ben-Hadad tried again at a town called Aphek. Another man of God showed up and told Ahab he would win the battle. They did, but God was mad at Ahab for letting Ben-Hadad go free. Now the prophet confirmed Ahab's life would soon end.

Sometime later, Ahab wanted a nearby vineyard owned by a man named Naboth. He asked Naboth for it, but Naboth refused. Ahab backed off. Jezebel found him and said, "What kind of a king are you? You take whatever you want." So she killed Naboth and took the vineyard from him.

Elijah sent word to Ahab. "Because of your awful deeds, dogs will lick up your blood and your wife's blood. Plus, all your descendants will be wiped out." But Ahab had a surprising reaction. He actually felt bad, repented, and fasted. God was pleased and delayed his death.

Three years later, the king of Judah, Jehoshaphat, went to see Ahab. He needed help to defeat the enemy in Ramoth Gilead. Jehoshaphat, a good king, wanted to seek advice from a prophet. Ahab brought four hundred of his own prophets, who all said, "Yes, yes, yes. Sounds good. You'll win!" Jehoshaphat found them strange. "Okay, do you have any real prophets of the Lord?"

Ahab reluctantly offered this one prophet named Micaiah, but Ahab said, "He never prophesies anything good."

Micaiah arrived and said, "You guys will definitely win, but these prophets are deceptive. Don't believe them." The prophets slapped him around and drug him off to prison. He yelled, "If you, King Ahab, return safely, then I'm not a real prophet."

Ahab did not return from the battle at Ramoth Gilead. During the fight, an archer fired off a random shot into the air, but God knew where it was going . . . right between the armor on King Ahab. He died just as the prophet predicted.

Son of a Bad King (1 KINGS 22:51-2 KINGS 1)

Ahab's son, Ahaziah, took over from his father, but he acted exactly like his mom and dad. He reigned for two years. God didn't like him because he worshiped the god Baal. Once, Ahaziah fell through a roof and was badly injured. He sent a messenger to consult his false god, but an angel interjected and told Elijah to go check on him.

Elijah intercepted the messenger and said, "Why are you asking some lame god to help the king? Ahaziah won't get out of this bed until he dies."

> John the Baptist wore similar clothing. That's why he's also known as an "Elijah."

The messenger went back and told the king what the man said. "What man?" Ahaziah questioned. "What did he look like?"

"He had a suit of hair and a leather belt."

Ahaziah knew who it was. "Elijah. Send fifty soldiers to go get him."

The fifty soldiers showed up to take Elijah. Fire fell from heaven and consumed them.

The king sent fifty more soldiers. More fire fell and killed them.

The king sent fifty more soldiers. This army captain asked Elijah nicely and respectfully. Elijah went with him.

Elijah arrived and repeated to Ahaziah what he said before: "Why are you seeking some god named Baal? You're going to die in that bed."

The king did die, and since he had no son, a man named Joram succeeded him as king.

Elijah Goes Up and Elisha Jumps In (2 KINGS 2–10; 2 CHRONICLES 21–22:9)

A group of prophets followed Elijah. They all knew what was about to happen. It was Elijah's last day on earth. He faced a river, took off his cloak, and struck the water. The water divided and Elijah walked across.

Elijah turned to Elisha and asked what he could do for him before he left.

Elisha said, "I want twice the spirit you have!"

Then a chariot of fire from heaven, led by horses, showed up and whisked Elijah to the sky. Only his cloak was left. Elisha took it and put it on.

Elisha began to do some amazing miracles. He healed a spring of poisoned water. A group of kids teased Elisha, calling him "Baldy," and two bears roared out of nowhere and taught them a lesson.

Elisha communicated a plan from God to Joram, the king, to defeat the Moabites by digging holes in the battleground and filling them with water. God made the Moabites think they were pools of blood and the Israel army was all dead, so they invaded the camp of Israel to take the leftover plunder. But the army was waiting for them and defeated them.

In a miracle very much like Elijah's, Elisha helped a widow replenish her olive oil supply to pay her debts.

He then raised a woman's son to life and cleansed a pot of stew that had a poison weed in it.

A man brought twenty loaves of bread to Elisha. Elisha wanted the people to have it, but there were one hundred in attendance. It didn't seem like enough, but Elisha promised it would fill them. It did, and they had some left over.

A commander of an army, named Naaman, had a skin disease called leprosy, and heard that Elisha did amazing things. Elisha agreed to help him; he told Naaman to wash himself seven times in the Jordan River. Naaman thought that was ridiculous—until he did it and was healed. Elisha even raised an ax head that had fallen into the river to the surface, just so the borrower could return the ax as he found it.

Elisha's miracle of bread is very much like Jesus' feeding of five thousand and four thousand. Every account said that everyone ate and was satisfied. Plus, there were even leftovers.

During a war between Israel and Aram, Elisha heard from God where the Arameans were camping and passed the information on to Israel. This infuriated the king of Aram, who sent an army to capture Elisha. Elisha's servant got nervous seeing the army surrounding their city. Elisha prayed the servant's eyes would be opened, and suddenly he saw a great angelic army all around them.

Elisha then prayed that the eyes of the army from Aram would be blind. In an instant, none of them could see. Elisha and his servant walked away unseen. Then he prayed their eyes would be opened. They were. Later, that army from Aram surrounded Samaria and cut off their food supply. God caused the Arameans to hear the sounds of chariots and horses grow so loud, they ran away scared, leaving all their gold and supplies.

Certainly, the miracles Elisha showed were twice as amazing, just as he asked.

Elisha had a man named Jehu anointed as king of the northern nation. Jehu killed Joram, the current king, with an arrow shot right through Joram's heart. He also killed Ahaziah, the king of Judah. Jehu found Jezebel, Ahab's wife, and trapped her in a tower. Jezebel's own servants tossed her out and she died on impact. Dogs, as predicted, licked up her blood. Jehu went on to wipe out all of Ahab's family.

Even though Jehu then killed all the servants of the god Baal, and destroyed many temples to other gods, he himself worshiped the golden calves in Bethel and Daniel. That didn't please God, but Jehu did stay in office for twenty-eight years.

More Bad Kings (2 KINGS 13, 14:23-29; 2 CHRONICLES 25-26:2)

The northern nation of Israel did not end well. Even all the work done by Elijah and Elisha—to prove there was a God—failed to bring them out of their sin and constant fascination with false gods and idols. King after king brought disaster on the nation.

Jehu's son, Jehoahaz, was evil, and God's anger burned against him. His army was reduced to nearly nothing by wars with the king of Aram. He died after being king for seventeen years.

Jehoash, Jehoahaz's son, reigned for sixteen years. He did visit Elisha while he was sick, who promised Jehoash three victories against the nation of Aram, but no more.

Soon after, Elisha died. What's cool about Elisha is that even after his death, he did miracles. When they threw his body into a tomb, it touched the remains of another dead man, who came to life and walked out.

After Jehoash, Jeroboam II, his son, became king. He reigned for a long time—forty-one years. Things just were not getting better. God saw all the misery the people in the Northern Kingdom experienced. It was time to send the Northern Kingdom a message.

God sent three prophets to them during the time Jeroboam II sat on the throne.

One was named Hosea. God used Hosea's marriage as an example of how it makes God feel when someone strays and finds other people to love. Hosea's message told of God's judgment if they loved other gods, but he offered a message of hope and love if they returned to God, just as Hosea's wife returned to him.

The second prophet was named Amos. He was a simple shepherd whose message to Israel was the same as

Hosea's, speaking of judgment and destruction. A priest from Bethel complained about Amos to Jeroboam II, wanting Amos kicked out, but Amos stayed strong and his warning did not waver.

The third and most famous prophet, Jonah, was known by his "fishy" story.

Man Overboard (JONAH 1-4)

The city of Nineveh was the capital of the Assyrian empire, which was growing in power. Despite their neglect of God, God still loved them. He wanted to send

a prophet to tell them about God's mercy and judgment. But the prophet God sent didn't want them to hear that message.

Jonah clearly heard from God: "Go to Nineveh and preach against their wickedness." But Jonah ran the other way, getting on a boat in Joppa to sail to Tarshish. God stirred up a storm to slow the boat down. The sailors on board all worshiped their gods, then realized the reason this storm struck was because of Jonah.

Jonah agreed to be thrown into the water so everyone could travel safely. When he hit the water, a giant fish swallowed him and vomited him up safely on the shore. Jonah understood what he had to do, even if he didn't want to do it.

Jonah walked across the city of Nineveh for three days, all while delivering a very simple message: "Forty more days and the city will be overthrown." The people panicked and prayed. Even the king heard and told everyone to seek God. The whole town—120,000 people—stopped their evil ways. God saw what happened to the people's hearts and did not destroy Nineveh.

But Jonah wasn't happy. He knew it was an evil city and it deserved punishment, but God told him, "I will be kind to whomever I want."

This Is the End (2 KINGS 15:8–31, 17)

The people of Israel, including the kings, stopped listening to the message of any of the prophets. Now began the long slide into the complete destruction of Israel. Politically, Israel was a mess.

After King Jeroboam II came his son, Zechariah, who held the throne for only six months until Shallum assassinated him. Shallum took over northern Israel for only one month, when Menahem assassinated him. Menahem reigned for ten years, but God didn't like how he led the people.

During this time, Assyria was growing into a superpower, led by a king named Pul, the Hebrew name for Tiglath-Pileser. Soon Israel would not be able to stand up to them.

Menahem's son, Pekahiah, took over when his father died and was king for two years. One of his chief officers, Pekah, assassinated him and took the throne. Pekah reigned for twenty years.

Around 740 BC, the king of Assyria, Tiglath-Pileser, took over Israel and scattered the people all over. Pekah was assassinated by Hoshea, who became the last king of Israel.

Hoshea reigned over practically nothing with all the nation in chaos. He was evil but lasted nine years. Eventually, Shalmaneser, the new king of Assyria, invaded Samaria, the capital, in 722 BC, and officially ended the era of the Northern Kingdom.

Why did this happen? The northern nation did not listen to the prophets God sent. They worshiped other gods, which said to God that they thought he wasn't powerful enough for them. God allowed them to be punished to show that their idols were worthless.

Assyria brought people from other nations into the northern area of Israel and allowed them to live there. They worshiped both the Lord and their own gods. But it doesn't work that way. God demands all our worship because he is the only God who is real. This disobedience continued for many generations to come.

God was patient with the Northern Kingdom, allowing it to exist for two hundred years. His patience, though, has limits. He would deal the same way with the Southern Kingdom of Judah, but thankfully, eight of those kings were good and followed the Lord. This kept them from facing judgment like the north, and they survived two hundred years longer.

Kings of Israel in Order
(931–722 BC)

- ☹ **Jeroboam,** a bad king for 22 years.
- ☹ **Nadab,** a bad king for 2 years.
- ☹ **Baasha,** a bad king for 24 years.
- ☹ **Elah,** a bad king for two years, killed by Zimri.
- ☹ **Zimri,** a bad king for 7 days.
- ☹ **Omri,** a bad king for 12 years.
- ☹☹ **Ahab,** a really bad king for 22 years.
- ☹ **Ahaziah,** a bad king of Israel for 2 years.
- ☹ **Joram,** a bad king for 12 years.
- ☹ **Jehoahaz,** a bad king for 17 years.
- ☹☹ **Jehoash,** an evil king for 16 years.
- ☹ **Jeroboam II,** a bad king for 41 years.
- ☹ **Zechariah,** a bad king for 6 months.
- ☹ **Shallum,** a bad king for 1 month.
- ☹ **Menahem,** a bad king for 10 years.
- ☹ **Pekahiah,** a bad king for 2 years.
- ☹ **Pekah,** a bad king for 20 years.
- ☹ **Hoshea,** a bad king for 9 years. Israel fell when Samaria moved in.

WHAT'S THE POINT?

▶ Politics can be mean and nasty. People get very selfish with power.

▶ God wants to be the only God in your life. He does not put up with other gods for very long.

▶ God can change history and destroy an entire nation. The northern nation lasted 210 years. That's less than the United States right now (over 245 years).

▶ Even the great people of God sometimes get weak, scared, and tired. They just need some rest.

11

The Southern Kingdom

1 KINGS; 2 KINGS; 2 CHRONICLES

 WHO'S WHO

- » **Rehoboam**—really messed things up by listening to his friends
- » **Asa**—the king with the fewest letters in his name
- » **Jehoshaphat**—the king with the most letters in his name
- » **Joash**—the youngest king in Israel's history
- » **Josiah**—the second-youngest king in Israel's history
- » **Hezekiah**—a really good king who saw shadows go backwards
- » **Isaiah**—a really major prophet
- » **Jeremiah**—a prophet who cares . . . and cries

WHERE ARE WE?

- » **Jerusalem**—where God lives in a temple, for now

INTERESTING STUFF IN THIS SECTION

» Joash was seven years old when he became king. Josiah was eight.

» The Southern Kingdom lasted 344 years, compared to the north's 210 years.

» Obadiah is the shortest book of the Old Testament.

» Jeremiah is considered the longest book of the Bible in terms of word count—33,000 words.

» At least eight prophets tried to turn Judah's sin around. They couldn't.

Hold That Throne (1 KINGS 12, 15, 22; 2 CHRONICLES 10-11, 13-21:4)

The Southern Kingdom, known as Judah, was created after the ten tribes to the north split off because they did not like Rehoboam as king. Only two tribes made up the Southern Kingdom—Benjamin and Judah. They controlled Jerusalem and the rightful temple and priests who worked there. Overall, they did more good than the Northern Kingdom, but they eventually disintegrated by following the same mistakes as the Northern Kingdom.

God kept one promise during this time. While the northern nation had random people on the throne, God kept the line of David intact on the throne in the south, just as he said it would be.

Rehoboam, the grandson of David, became king at forty-one years old. He lasted seventeen years. He was an awful king. He plunged Judah even further into unrest by setting up high places, sacred stones, shrines, and poles to worship other gods, and committing all kinds of detestable practices. God allowed Egypt, led by Shishak the king, to attack Jerusalem and carry away their precious gold. Eventually, Rehoboam died and his son Abijah took over.

Abijah failed like Rehoboam. He did have a little battle with Jeroboam, proclaiming to the Israelites that Judah had the line of David, the temple, and the priests. God pushed Israel back and Abijah won. He only lasted three years as king until his son, Asa, became king.

Asa was king for forty-one years and actually turned things around. He kicked out the religious leaders of the false gods and got rid of many idols. Asa even removed his grandmother from her position because she also worshiped terrible idols. God blessed Asa with silver and gold. Unfortunately, Asa used those resources to pay the nation of Aram to protect him against Israel and its king, Baasha. A prophet scolded him for relying on Aram and not God for help.

His son Jehoshaphat became king of Judah when Asa died from a disease in his feet. He too was a very good king, doing everything his father ever taught him. God was pleased with Jehoshaphat because Jehoshaphat sought God's will in everything; however, Jehoshaphat didn't remove all the idols from Judah. Jehoshaphat had priests walk throughout Judah and read the book of the law to everyone so they could hear the Word of God. He also appointed judges and priests to enforce the law of God in their areas. God gave Jehoshaphat victory when he went up against the Ammonites and Moabites. Then he made an alliance with King Ahaziah of Israel to build a fleet of ships, but God didn't like him making treaties with an evil king, so the ships were destroyed. When Jehoshaphat died after twenty-five years as king, his son Jehoram became king at the age of thirty-five.

Jehoram was bad. He was more like the evil King Ahab than his good father, Jehoshaphat. He even married a daughter of Ahab and brought all those evil idols back into Judah. God didn't judge the nation yet. Jehoram died after eight years of being king.

His son, Ahaziah, became king at the age of twenty-two. He was one of two kings named Ahaziah in the Bible. This Ahaziah reigned for only one year, which was good, because he was bad too.

A Seven-Year-Old King (2 KINGS 11-12; 2 CHRONICLES 22-24)

Athaliah, Ahaziah's mother, was furious to hear her son was dead, so she killed her whole family. That's right—her whole family. But Jehosheba, the daughter of Jehoram and sister of Ahaziah, had hidden one of Ahaziah's sons, Joash, for six years. The line of David was preserved. God waited until the right time to restore the throne.

When Joash was seven, Jehoiada, a priest who wanted to see the right king from the line of David on the throne of Judah, sent for the commanders of the army to come to the temple. They shouted, "Joash is king!" and Jehoiada

put a crown on him. Athaliah heard the noise and cried, "Treason!" Jehoiada had her killed.

A new era began for Judah, a good one. Jehoiada had all those terrible temples to Baal destroyed. Everything was smashed to pieces.

Joash took the throne . . . at seven years old! Now, a seven-year-old can't run a nation, so his teacher, Jehoiada, showed him how, guiding him correctly in God's ways. Joash remained king for forty years!

One of the first things Joash did was make sure the temple was repaired. Over time, nobody fixed the damages to Solomon's temple, but Joash wanted to honor God with a beautiful home. Joash asked all the priests why this was happening. They apologized and made sure it got fixed. Carpenters and builders went to work.

Joash wasn't perfect. After Jehoiada died, the people returned to their false gods and idols. Prophets came to warn the people, but no one listened. Joash should have asked the Lord for help, but instead he tried to pay his enemy, the king of Aram, to stay away. Sadly, he was assassinated by his officials. His son Amaziah took over as king.

Two-for-One Prophets (ISAIAH AND MICAH)

Two prophets—Isaiah and Micah—arose in the south during this time; they focused their message on the one true God.

Isaiah prophesied during the reign of four kings. These four kings were on the throne for a combined 119 years, so Isaiah probably prophesied during portions of their reigns. Either way, that meant he heard from God and prophesied for around eighty years, during the reigns of three good kings and one bad one.

Isaiah's prophecies cover a lot of material—sixty-six chapters—making it one of the most important books of the Bible. He guided Judah during an important time, making sure they kept their focus on God. His book also contains incredible prophecies (7:14; 9:6) pointing to the birth of the Messiah, Jesus, and also incredibly detailed prophecies pointing to his death on the cross (chapters 52–54). In all, over forty prophecies in Isaiah were fulfilled by Jesus.

Another prophet also emerged during this time: Micah. He prophesied during the reigns of three of the same kings as Isaiah. Micah's words from God pronounce judgment on Samaria and Jerusalem, Israel and Judah. The political and religious leaders were scolded for being bad.

Like Isaiah, Micah also included a famous prophecy pointing to the city of Bethlehem (5:2), announcing that out of Bethlehem would come a Messiah who will rule over Israel, and he will come from ancient times (meaning he's been around a long time . . . like, forever).

Two Good Kings Out of Three Ain't Bad
(2 KINGS 14–17; 2 CHRONICLES 25–28)

Amaziah was a good king, like his dad, Joash, and David. He executed the officials who killed his father. But like many of the kings before him, he didn't get rid of the worship places to the idols and false gods. Instead, he set up his own gods in the temple and worshiped them. He didn't listen to the warnings from prophets.

One time, in a huge battle, Amaziah's army defeated ten thousand Edomites. Feeling impressed by himself, Amaziah decided to attack Israel to the north (they were still a nation during this time). Jehoash, the king of Israel, tried to reason with Amaziah, but Amaziah pushed his army forward. Amaziah lost and Jehoash broke into Jerusalem, stealing many valuables.

Amaziah was the king for twenty-five years. Just like with his father, a group wanted to kill him. He ran away and hid, but they found him and killed him. His son, Azariah, became king at the age of sixteen years old.

Azariah went by another name, Uzziah. He stayed on the throne for a long time—fifty-two years—and was very close to the prophets Zechariah and Isaiah. Uzziah did what was right in God's eyes and sought God's direction constantly. He made towers around Jerusalem and developed machine guns that fired arrows. But near the end of his life, Uzziah went into God's temple to burn incense to a false god. The priests confronted him, and God gave Uzziah leprosy to his death.

Jotham, Uzziah's son, took over. He did a good job, like his father, but never entered the temple. For his sixteen years in power, Jotham also did nothing about those hidden worship centers to other gods. Jotham had some victories and walked steadfastly with the Lord, and God considered him a good king, but not perfect.

Ahaz, Jotham's son, took over, but he really messed up. He was more like those evil kings in the north, actively taking part in all those sacrifices and worship ceremonies to false gods. This did not make God happy. In fact, God allowed Judah's enemies to overpower them, such as Israel to the north, the Edomites, and the Philistines. The king of Aram also marched right up to Jerusalem and set up a barricade around them. Ahaz didn't turn to God for help. He turned to Assyria, offering them silver and gold. Assyria saved them.

Ahaz went up to Damascus to thank Tiglath-Pileser, king of Assyria, for their help. While there, he saw a temple to a god that he liked and had his priest, Uriah, draw a sketch of it. Uriah built the terrible altar inside God's holy temple! Ahaz showed up and worshiped a false god right in the place where God should be worshiped. Eventually, Ahaz died, and his son, Hezekiah, took over. Hezekiah was a very good king.

All Hail Hezekiah (2 KINGS 18–20; 2 CHRONICLES 29–32)

Hezekiah was twenty-five years old when he became king, and he lasted twenty-nine years. During that time, he did what few other kings before him did—he smashed those altars to false gods. Finally! He served the Lord with everything in his heart and God loved it, allowing him to be successful in many things. Hezekiah made sure Passover was celebrated, which had not happened in Jerusalem for decades! It was so successful, they extended it an extra week. People gave so much to God, piles of donations sat at the temple. The temple got a nice makeover.

Hezekiah turned away from the king of Assyria and refused to serve him. Even while Shalmaneser, king of Assyria, marched into Samaria during its final hours, scattering all the northern tribes far away, Hezekiah did not back down in Judah.

Then Assyria pushed into Judah, Hezekiah's territory. Hezekiah panicked. He paid the Assyrian king all the silver and gold from the temple. This didn't stop Assyria. They wanted more and came right up to Jerusalem. Sennacherib, the new king of Assyria, called for Hezekiah. Hezekiah's administrators went out to meet the Assyrian.

Hezekiah is famous for the building of a tunnel from the Gihon spring to the Pool of Siloam inside Jerusalem to provide a water supply for the city during the time of a siege. The tunnel, which was dug from opposite ends, is an amazing engineering feat. Today, tourists can walk the full length of the tunnel.

"Don't listen to Hezekiah. He doesn't know what's best for you. Surrender to me. Trust in me, not in your God. No God can stop my army!"

When the administrators told this to Hezekiah, he broke down and cried in the temple. Isaiah the prophet told them not to listen to this king. Isaiah said, "God will make him to return to his country and be cut down with a sword." Hezekiah prayed for God to save them and to show the world that the Lord was the only God. Isaiah confirmed that God heard Hezekiah's prayer.

That night, an angel of death moved across the Assyrian camp and killed 180,000 soldiers. Sennacherib went back to his country and, while worshiping some false god, his sons killed him with a sword, just as Isaiah prophesied.

Hezekiah became very ill—so ill he almost died. Isaiah even confirmed he would die. But Hezekiah still prayed, turning his face to God and pleading to live. Isaiah returned and told Hezekiah that God heard the prayer, and Hezekiah would live for another fifteen years. Isaiah treated the illness with figs and said God would give Hezekiah a sign: The shadow on the steps would go the opposite it usually does when the sun goes down. Hezekiah looked out and saw it. The shadow moved differently than it ever had before.

But Hezekiah wasn't perfect. A rising force in the north, Babylon, sent ambassadors to Jerusalem to meet Hezekiah. Hezekiah did something prideful—he showed off all his gold in the temple. Isaiah told him that one day those Babylonians would return and take all the gold and silver from his future descendants. While Hezekiah would enjoy peace during his lifetime, the future residents of Jerusalem would not.

Hezekiah died and his son Manasseh took over as king.

Bad Times, Good Times (2 KINGS 21–22; 2 CHRONICLES 33–36)

Manasseh was twelve years old when he became king, and lasted fifty-five years on the throne. He was a bad boy, more evil than the evil nations around them. He rebuilt all the shrines and high places to foreign gods that his father, Hezekiah, tore down, putting many of them right in God's temple! Manasseh even sacrificed his own son to a god and talked to astrologers and people who claimed they talked to the dead. He shed so much innocent blood, God couldn't wait to get him off the throne. When Manasseh was captured by Assyria, he repented and returned to Jerusalem and made some positive changes. But not enough to make up for all the bad he did.

Sadly, his son Amon did just as much evil, and God allowed him to be assassinated after only two years. Then came the last good king of Judah's history—Josiah.

Josiah was another child king, eight years old when he started. When he grew up, Josiah really started to make positive changes in Judah. As the temple was getting cleaned up and repaired, a priest named Hilkiah found the book of the law in the temple. This contained all the writings of the Bible from Moses to their present day. Apparently, nobody was reading it or knew it was lost.

Hilkiah and the king's secretary, Shebna, brought it to King Josiah and read it. The king cried and demanded that the priests examine everything they needed to do to keep the Lord from getting angry at them. They went to the temple and cleared out all the worthless idols Amon put in there. He made sure the people celebrated a huge Passover. Josiah even had all the high places Solomon had built—which nobody had destroyed for hundreds of years—completely demolished. He made sure those idol worshipers didn't rebuild their temples by killing all their priests. God loved Josiah for how much he cleaned up Judah, removing all those detestable gods. Sadly, Josiah died by an arrow when he led his army out to fight Necho, king of Egypt, in a battle. His son, Jehoahaz, became king but lasted only three months when

Necho put him in chains and put Eliakim, Jehoahaz's son, on the throne. Egypt demanded money from Judah, holding it hostage. Heavy taxes were demanded from the people to pay off Egypt.

A Parade of Prophets (NAHUM, JOEL, HABAKKUK, OBADIAH, ZEPHANIAH, JEREMIAH)

God really needed to get a message to his people in Judah. Assyria had wiped out the north, and now the south was doomed. Since they repeated the same sins as the north, God sent prophets to deliver a similar message. Six prophets spoke during the time of these final kings.

Nahum expressed God's anger toward Nineveh. Nineveh had turned back to its evil ways after Jonah's visit. Nahum warned them of the coming doom they would face as another nation grew into a great power (Babylon).

Joel likened God's wrath to a swarm of locusts buzzing into a land and eating up everything in sight. The swarm could have been actual locusts (like in the plagues of Exodus) or an army invading the land. Either way, God allowed it to happen to repay them for their sins.

Habakkuk saw how God was building up another nation (Babylon) that was more evil and more destructive than Assyria, and wondered how God could allow a bad nation to punish Judah. God's answer: "You must trust me!" Habakkuk could only respond by praising God.

Zephaniah pronounced judgment not only on Jerusalem and Judah, but also on other nations in the region—Philistia, Moab, Assyria, and others. Judah may be God's favorite, but he holds them up to the same standard as other nations.

Obadiah had a specific message for the nation of Edom only. Edom descended from Esau, and God pronounced a final judgment on them. He could not tolerate them any longer.

Finally, there's Jeremiah, one of the greatest prophets of the Old Testament. His book covers a lot of time—fifty to sixty years. He had a lot to say over a long period.

Jeremiah came from a line of priests, and God told him that ever since Jeremiah was born, God knew what he would do. Jeremiah, many times putting himself at risk, stood up to the priests and leaders to tell them very clearly that God was not happy with them. Nobody listened to his message; instead, they punished him.

Jeremiah received the nickname of the "weeping prophet" because he cried so much watching God's great nation deteriorate. Jeremiah put his life on the line to save Jerusalem and face the leaders who were destroying it.

The End . . . for Now (2 KINGS 23-24; 2 CHRONICLES 36)

Eliakim's son, Jehoiakim, became king and, like his father, did evil. During his reign of eleven years, another superpower conquered Assyria and pushed back Egypt. The nation was Babylon, led by its king, Nebuchadnezzar. Babylon wanted Judah and Jerusalem next. Jeremiah wrote the king of Judah, Jehoiakim, a scroll of warning. Jehoiakim cut it into pieces and tossed it into the fire.

After Jehoiakim came his son, Jehoiachin (don't you love these names). He was only eighteen when he started and, like his grandfather, lasted only three months. Nebuchadnezzar stormed the city and took him prisoner, shipping him back to their capital in Babylon. Nebuchadnezzar put another king on the throne, Zedekiah, who lasted eleven years. His job was to do whatever Babylon told him to do.

Jeremiah kept stepping in to stop Judah from worshiping other gods and warning them of God's judgment, but they locked Jeremiah in prison and chains and tossed him into an underground well.

Kings of Judah in Order
(931–586 BC)

☹ **Rehoboam** bad king for 17 years.

☹ **Abijah**, son of Rehboam; a bad king for 3 years.

☺ **Asa**, a good king for 41 years!

☺ **Jehoshaphat**, a good king of Judah for 25 years!

☹ **Jehoram**, a bad king for 8 years.

☹ **Ahaziah**, a bad king for 1 year.

☹ **Athaliah**, a bad grandma queen for 6 years.

☺ **Joash**, a good king starting at seven years old for 38 years!

☺ **Amaziah**, a good king for 29 years!

☺ **Azariah**, a good king starting at 16 years old for 52 years!

☺ **Jotham**, a good king for 16 years!

☹ **Ahaz**, a bad king for 16 years.

☺ **Hezekiah** was a good king for 29 years!

☹☹ **Manasseh**, a really bad king for 55 years.

☹ **Amon**, a bad king for 22 years.

☺ **Josiah**, a good king for 32 years starting at 8 years old!

☹ **Jehoahaz**, a bad king for 3 months.

☹ **Jehoiakim**, a bad king for 11 years.

☹ **Jehoachin**, a bad king for 3 months.

☹ **Mattaniah**, a bad king for 11 years. Name changed to Zedekiah. Babylon defeated Judah and moved the people out.

Nebuchadnezzar shipped out the best and the brightest in Judah to Babylon (more on that in the next chapter), leaving Jerusalem practically empty. Zedekiah didn't listen to his bosses in Babylon and, as punishment, the whole army came down to attack. Zedekiah asked Jeremiah to speak to God to stop the enemy, but God could not be persuaded to stop them. Zedekiah was forced to watch the slaughter of his sons, and then he was blinded and taken to Babylon as a captive. Jeremiah had correctly prophesied that all of Israel would be in captivity for seventy years.

Jerusalem's walls were torn down, and the temple—the beautiful temple Solomon built—was completely destroyed. Jeremiah's book Lamentations is a song of sorrow as he saw the end of Jerusalem.

Nebuchadnezzar put a guy named Gedaliah in charge, then left Judah for good. Gedaliah did his best to bring peace, but he was assassinated by a group of men from Judah, leaving Jerusalem without any leadership.

Jeremiah and all the prophets made prophecies

about Israel and Judah's complete destruction. But every dire prophecy ended on a note of hope. God always promised that he would restore the nation to peace.

And that's exactly what God did, seventy years later.

WHAT'S THE POINT?

▶ God shows lots of grace and patience with us, but eventually he says, "You're grounded!" We won't like the punishment; it's designed to make us think about what we've done, repent, and seek reconciliation.

▶ Our nation's leadership is important. They won't be perfect and they will make mistakes, but the main question is, Do they follow God?

▶ The good kings tried to remove the bad idols from the world. We must do that in our world.

▶ Are you sad about how the world is, or do you just shrug and say, "Oh well"?

12

Home Again

DANIEL; EZRA; NEHEMIAH; ESTHER

 WHO'S WHO

- » **Daniel**—every lion's best friend
- » **Shadrach, Meshach, Abednego**—three "fired up" friends
- » **King Nebuchadnezzar**—a bad Babylonian king who met the real King
- » **Zerubbabel**—a builder and general contractor
- » **Ezra**—one tough priest
- » **Nehemiah**—a drink taster and wall builder
- » **Esther**—a beautiful and smart queen who saves her people
- » **King Cyrus**—a Persian king who finds himself the answer to a prophecy

165

WHERE ARE WE?

» **Jerusalem**—a desolate city that got an extreme makeover

» **Babylon**—the once-powerful kingdom falls in one night

 INTERESTING STUFF IN THIS SECTION

» Daniel is one of the few people in the Bible that we hear nothing negative about.

» The Bible mentions the names of only two angels (besides Satan)—Michael and Gabriel. Daniel was visited by both of them.

» God is not mentioned by name in the book of Esther, but his presence is known because of the way so many things fall into place.

» Haggai's name is pronounced "ha-guy."

» Zechariah and Ezekiel have some of the strangest visions in the Bible. Visions weren't always easy to understand, but they were sometimes designed to show the power and mystery of God.

» Malachi wins the honor of being the last book of the Old Testament. It was written last, too.

Water and Veggies, Please! (DANIEL 1-2)

After Babylon invaded Jerusalem, they removed groups of people they thought were cooler than everyone else—people who they thought were the smartest, most handsome, most beautiful, and best leaders.

Babylon wanted to turn them into Babylonians by teaching them their language and literature. To do so, they gave them the best food and drink as part of a three-year training program.

Four men amongst the exiles were named Daniel, Hananiah, Mishael, and Azariah. The official in charge of the men renamed those last three Shadrach, Meshach, and Abednego. All four saw through the purpose of this program and refused the food, preferring to eat for ten days a diet of veggies and water.

The official was nervous, but saw, after ten days, that they looked good. God gave them incredible knowledge and understanding. Daniel could interpret visions and dreams. King Nebuchadnezzar said these four guys were ten times smarter than the magicians and wise men in his court.

Then, one night, Nebuchadnezzar had a dream that really bothered him. His magicians, sorcerers, and astrologers asked him to tell them the dream so they could interpret it. Nebuchadnezzar said no. "You guys arc so smart, you tell me the dream!" They thought this was a joke, but it wasn't. In fact, if nobody could tell him his own dream, they would all die. But someone remembered Daniel's ability.

> These wise men were the ancestors of the same wise men who visited Jesus. They knew the Scriptures because the Jews once lived among them in exile.

Daniel prayed and fasted and came before Nebuchadnezzar. "Please don't klll anyone. My God has told me your dream." Then Daniel precisely revealed the dream of a statue with four parts—gold, silver, iron, and clay. The statue represented the kings God has, and will, put in power over the centuries.

King Nebuchadnezzar fell on his face. Daniel did it. The wise men of Babylon were saved. "Your God is the God of gods and Lord of kings," Nebuchadnezzar said. As a result, Daniel got a promotion as the leader of all the wise men.

Hot Times in Babylon Tonight (DANIEL 3)

The king eventually forgot his statement glorifying God and decided to glorify himself with a giant statue and told people to worship it. Every time music started playing, everyone had to pray in the direction of this gold statue. If they did not, they would be thrown into a blazing furnace.

Three men refused to bow—Shadrach, Meshach, and Abednego. They were arrested and brought to the furnace. Nebuchadnezzar said, "What god can save you now?" The men replied, "Our God can save us from a hot furnace, but even if he doesn't, we aren't bowing to your god."

The soldiers took Shadrach, Meshach, and Abednego to the furnace, which was so hot, soldiers died just getting close to it. But Shadrach, Meshach, and Abednego didn't die. In fact, they walked around inside the furnace. Nebuchadnezzar looked closer and thought he saw a fourth man walking around. An angel? God?

He ordered them to come out. Nothing on Shadrach, Meshach, and Abednego's bodies was even slightly burnt. They didn't even smell of smoke! "Your God is greater than anything else," Nebuchadnezzar said. But did the king really believe it yet?

A Crazy Dream (DANIEL 4)

Nebuchadnezzar had another dream and called Daniel. This time he said the dream out loud. It dealt with a tree, its leaves, and animals that lived around it. The tree was cut down and the animals scattered.

Daniel carefully gave Nebuchadnezzar the bad news. "You are that tree, and one day you will lose your mind. You will be driven away from the people and live with wild animals."

Twelve months later, Nebuchadnezzar walked out on his porch and looked at his great kingdom. Pridefully, he said, "This all happened because I'm a mighty king." Immediately, a voice from heaven called him out and kicked him out of Babylon.

Nebuchadnezzar lived like a wild animal his hair grew like feathers, his nails like long claws. Finally, Nebuchadnezzar turned to heaven and glorified God over every other god. His sanity returned when he became humble.

Writing on the Wall (DANIEL 5)

Belshazzar, son of Nebuchadnezzar, later became king of Babylon, and he decided to throw a huge party. During the party, he asked for the gold and silver goblets Nebuchadnezzar took from the Jewish temple. He wanted to drink from them during the party.

As they partied, a human hand began writing on a wall in the room. It was spooky! They saw the words that were written but didn't understand the meaning. Belshazzar promised riches and power to anyone who could interpret. Somebody called the great code-breaker: Daniel.

Daniel arrived and rejected any reward for his services. He looked at the four words, which read, *Mene, Mene, Tekel, Parsin*. Daniel knew those words. All of them dealt with numbers, weights, and measurements.

Daniel shook his head. "God has weighed your bad deeds against your good and you have come up short."

That night, in 539 BC, Persia attacked Babylon and took over the city of Babylon. Belshazzar was killed. Darius the Mede took over. The Persian reign began.

The Lions Sleep Tonight (DANIEL 6-12)

D arius appointed his own leaders to rule through the kingdom. He actually liked Daniel and gave him a position over those leaders. He did so well that other administrators in the Persian kingdom got jealous. They tried to find a way to trap him.

The administrators came up with a law that said every time anyone prays to anyone other than King Darius, they would be thrown into a lions' den. Darius signed the law.

Daniel heard about the law, pushed open his windows, and loudly prayed to the real God. He was arrested and brought to Darius, who was sad. He really liked Daniel, but a rule was a rule and Daniel had to pay.

Darius hoped Daniel's God would save him as Daniel was thrown into the pit of lions. Darius couldn't sleep that night.

Early in the morning, Darius had the pit opened, where he found Daniel alive. "Last night, an angel shut the mouths of the lions so they could not hurt me."

Darius declared Daniel's God the God of all gods and threw those people who tried to kill Daniel into the same lions' den. Immediately, they were devoured by the hungry lions.

Daniel lived on, having many visions and visits from two angels, Michael and Gabriel. The information he received told of future events and warnings of judgment on the world. Many still interpret his visions today as signs of the end times to come.

The Prophets Nailed It (EZEKIEL, ISAIAH)

Jeremiah correctly prophesied that the people of Israel would be in captivity under Babylon for seventy years (25:11). Then, he said, Babylon would be punished (25:12). Then Jeremiah said the Jews would return to Jerusalem (29:10). Jeremiah died in Egypt, where he was taken by his own people.

Ezekiel the prophet spoke the words and warnings from God during the last portion of Jeremiah's time. Ezekiel was around before the third and final Babylonian invasion, trying to warn the people of Jerusalem of their sin. He lived in exile, making visionary journeys to Jerusalem and seeing wild, incredible things, and predicted a return from exile and a future restoration of Israel.

Over one hundred years before Persia came to power, the prophet Isaiah said, three times in three verses, that a ruler named Cyrus would be God's "righteousness," and would be used to rebuild Jerusalem. When Persia beat Babylon, that's exactly what happened. Persia allowed Israel to move back to Jerusalem and restore their city.

Jerusalem 2.0 (EZRA 1–6; HAGGAI; ZECHARIAH)

During the reign of Cyrus, the king of Persia, Zerubbabel led the first group of exiles back to Jerusalem to start the rebuilding process around 538–536 BC. Cyrus gave them a permission slip and a building permit to travel back to their homeland. Over forty thousand people took the opportunity to return home. They carried back the items stolen from their temple.

Their first priority was to build an altar so sacrifices could continue. The Levites joined the effort to make sure everything lined up biblically so they could celebrate the feasts. A man named Joshua was assigned the position of high priest.

Their next priority was to lay the foundation of the temple. The foundation is the most important part to make sure the building will stand. People celebrated, sang, and worshiped God, and some wept when they remembered the former glory of the temple.

However, there's always opposition when something good for God gets underway. Outsiders who lived in Jerusalem before the return of the exiles didn't like their land taken away from them. They started rumors and lies. They bribed officials and created a lot of doubt and chaos. They sent word to the king of the time, saying things like, "These people are rebels and they'll only try to bring you down." The king shut the rebuilding down.

Around 520 BC, when the building stalled, two prophets spoke up. Haggai warned that unless the people moved forward, there would be a drought. His words stirred the spirit of Zerubbabel. Four times Haggai encouraged Zerubbabel to press on despite the opposition he heard.

Zechariah also prophesied during this time, and his visions were wild. He saw a man on a horse amongst myrtle trees, a man with a measuring stick, a flying scroll, a woman in a basket, and four chariots.

What did all this mean? God wanted the people to return to worshiping God. It was not going to happen by might and power, but by God's Spirit. He promised to send someone to unite Israel. This person would be pierced and die to cleanse everyone of their sins. In many ways, this Promised One would be a shepherd to guide the people and a king to rule over them.

Yes, the prophets were preparing the people for Jesus, who would not come for another four to five hundred years.

Finally, the confusion was cleared up and the building process continued. King Darius of Persia proclaimed that Cyrus did give permission for the Israelites to rebuild, and nothing could stop them. In fact, if anyone tried, they would be executed. The temple was completed, and a Passover celebration was held.

Ezra and Nehemiah Come to Town (EZRA 7–10; NEHEMIAH)

In 458 BC, the priest Ezra came from Babylon to Israel with a new wave of exiles returning home during the reign of Artaxerxes. Ezra had the gift of teaching, and his wisdom would bring great changes to Israel. He saw the

Israelites marrying people from outside Israel, and bringing their god worship back into Jerusalem.

Ezra preached to the people, who realized their sin and confessed. Many dedicated themselves to God and keeping his commands.

Around 444 BC, Nehemiah worked as a cupbearer for King Artaxerxes. His job was to sip the king's drink to make sure it wasn't poisoned. That made him very close to the king. One day, Artaxerxes saw that Nehemiah was sad. He asked why.

Nehemiah had heard news about Jerusalem. The wall surrounding the city was down, making it exposed to enemies. The king gave him permission and money to return to Jerusalem and rebuild the wall.

Nehemiah gathered up all the people to rebuild sections of the wall closest to them. They also worked on the gates so people could safely enter and exit the city.

As with anything for God, opposition rose to stop the building process. Three men—Sanballat, Tobiah, and Geshem—began to spread rumors and make threats. Guards were posted to stop any attacks.

Meanwhile, Nehemiah, now governor of Jerusalem, helped the poor people who tried to survive while building the wall. He escaped assassination from his enemies.

Despite all this, the wall was completed in record time—fifty-two days!

Ezra, meanwhile, read from the book of the law daily to the people. Leadership was put into place, starting with the priests. The Israelites confessed their sins and dedicated themselves to God. They made promises to live for God! They dedicated the wall to God with choirs singing and sacrifices made.

Nehemiah turned everything over to his brother and returned back to his cupbearer job. But it didn't take long until everything fell apart again. Around 433 BC, Nehemiah heard of foreigners living in the temple, marriages occurring with outsiders, and the return of worshiping idols. (Outsiders were those who worshiped other gods, not people who were racially different.) Nehemiah angrily came back and turned things around.

Esther, the Beauty Queen (ESTHER)

Another important story happened in Persia that could have been very deadly for the Israelites around 485 BC. The king, Xerxes, threw a huge seven-day party to celebrate his kingdom. He asked for his wife, Queen Vashti, to come out so he could show her off to his friends. When she refused, he began to look for another wife.

A beauty contest was held to find the best wife for Xerxes. A man named Mordecai had a cousin named Hadassah, whom he adopted when her parents died. She also went by the name Esther. Esther entered the contest and made it to the final rounds. However, she never told anyone she was Jewish.

After a year of spa treatments and beauty makeovers, Esther won the king's hand and became queen of Persia. Mordecai, meanwhile, heard of a conspiracy to kill the king, and alerted the guards, who arrested the assassins.

Haman worked closely with the king as his advisor. Haman didn't like Mordecai because Mordecai never bowed when Haman walked by, like everyone else did. Mordecai bowed only to God. Haman heard Mordecai was a Jew, so he tricked the king into signing an order for the Persians to kill all the Jews on a certain date.

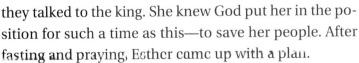

Mordecai came to Esther, asking her to plead with the king for help. But even queens had to be careful how they talked to the king. She knew God put her in the position for such a time as this—to save her people. After fasting and praying, Esther came up with a plan.

Xerxes saw Esther in his court and asked her if there was anything she wanted. Esther invited Xerxes to a banquet she would put on in his honor. Haman was invited, too. The banquet was a success, and Xerxes again asked Esther if there was anything she wanted. She said yes—another banquet. Haman could come to that, too.

Haman, feeling really good about himself, prepared a huge pole to kill Mordecai from—it was, like, seventy-five feet high!

Xerxes couldn't sleep one night so he had the boring historical records read to him. The records reminded him of the great thing Mordecai did to save his life. He asked Haman what the best way was to honor a great person. Haman thought the king was talking about him, so he said, "Parade the man around on a horse while it's being led through the streets by someone yelling how great the man on the horse is." Xerxes loved that idea. He told Haman to lead Mordecai around on a horse and proclaim his greatness.

Haman did, but it made him so angry. He told his family he couldn't wait to kill Mordecai. But right now, it was banquet time.

At the banquet, Xerxes asked a third time for Esther to share whatever request was on her heart. Esther made the announcement.

"Spare my people! Someone has tricked you into signing an order to kill them all!"

Xerxes was shocked. "Who tricked me?"

"This vile man—Haman!"

Xerxes couldn't believe it. His trusted assistant. Xerxes stepped out into the garden. Meanwhile, Haman pleaded with Esther, falling on the couch where Esther sat. From Xerxes' point of view, it looked like Haman was attacking his
wife. Xerxes ordered Haman to be killed. Someone suggested using the pole Haman had just built (you know, the one for Mordecai). Xerxes thought that was a good idea, and Haman was executed.

Now Mordecai became the king's second-in-command, and the group came up with an idea to save the Jews. The king made another rule—the Jews could fight back. When the people tried to kill the Jews according to Haman's law, the Jews defended themselves according to Mordecai's rule. No Jews died.

Esther, to this day, is honored through a holiday named Purim.

The Last Words (MALACHI)

As Jerusalem and Israel began the rebuilding process, priests and prophets worked to stop repeating the same sins that got the nation into trouble with God in the first place.

The last prophet to speak to Israel for God was Malachi, around the time of 420 BC. God was not happy with the priests and the kinds of sacrifices they offered. Instead of perfect sacrifices, they got rid of the blind, crippled, or diseased animals. They did not give God their best. The priests were poor examples of godly worship leaders to the people.

Many did not give their offerings to the fullest. *Tithe* means 10 percent, and the people gave less. In God's eyes, that's robbery. The people were stealing what belonged to God. The tithe was a requirement of the law. Christians today are not required to tithe; instead, they should give out of their love and thankfulness for God's gift of his Son.

God declared that he does not change. He always was a God of mercy and judgment. He forgave but he also punished. The door was always open for the people to humble themselves and return to him. God always promises to spare his people if they confess and humble themselves.

God made a promise to Israel. He would send a messenger to the people's hearts. Like a refinery, he would burn off all the sinful dirt. Like a laundry soap, he would wash them clean of sin.

This man would be a prophet in the likes of Elijah. His job would be to turn the people's hearts to their families and to God.

This man was John the Baptist, who pointed people to the coming Messiah, Jesus.

Many looked forward to this man's arrival, and it finally occurred, four hundred years later.

WHAT'S THE POINT?

► The book of Esther proves that God is always working behind the scenes, making events and circumstances move toward his purposes.

► In only moments, God has the power to take down a nation and bring up a new one.

► God can shut the mouths of lions and people around you if they want to hurt you.

► History is HIS-story. God determines history to fit his purpose.

13

He's Here

MATTHEW 1-2; LUKE 1-2

 WHO'S WHO

» **Zechariah**—John the Baptist's dad, who was put on mute

» **Elizabeth**—John the Baptist's mom

» **Gabriel**—an angel who delivers messages from heaven

» **Mary**—Jesus' mom and God's loyal servant

» **Joseph**—Jesus' earthly dad and a big dreamer

» **Jesus**—God who comes to earth as a baby

» **Wise men**—very smart guys who bring birthday presents to Jesus

» **Herod**—a king who hated to hear that another king was born in town

» **Shepherds**—workers on the night shift who get a concert sung by angels

WHERE ARE WE?

» **Nazareth**—a village in the mountains where Mary and Joseph met

» **Bethlehem**—a little town just like the song says

» **Egypt**—Jesus' family hid there just like families in the Old Testament did

INTERESTING STUFF IN THIS SECTION

» Christmas or Christ Mass means "a gathering to celebrate Jesus."

» A Messiah is someone who saves people from their sins. *Christ* is another name for the word *Messiah*.

» Joseph has the record for the most dreams in the Bible: four.

» Gabriel is a messenger angel. He delivered important messages to Daniel, Zechariah, and Mary.

» We don't know if there were only three wise men. We think that because there were three gifts, there were only three men, but two could have brought gold, five frankincense, and three myrrh, for example.

Zechariah Takes a Time-Out (LUKE 1:1-25)

Around 7 BC, a priest named Zechariah worked the temple in Jerusalem. He and his wife, Elizabeth, could not have any children. While Zechariah burned incense in the temple, the angel Gabriel appeared and told

him that he and his wife would have a son and to name him John. This boy would be filled with the Holy Spirit before he was born!

Zechariah hesitated, asking how this could happen, since they were getting very old. Gabriel said Zechariah would not be able to speak because he doubted.

He walked out of the temple and the people were amazed. He couldn't talk! They knew he had seen something that took his voice away.

Later, Elizabeth did get pregnant. Gabriel was right.

Mary Knows (LUKE 1:26–56)

Six months later, in Nazareth, a small town in the mountain region of Galilee, a young woman named Mary lived. She was engaged to a man named Joseph. Gabriel suddenly appeared to her and said, "Hello, young lady, loved by God. The Lord is with you." These words shook her. Then Gabriel told her the news.

"God has a special plan for you. You will give birth to a child and call him Jesus. He's great because he's the Son of God, and he will sit on the throne of David forever."

Prophecy fulfilled: "Therefore the Lord himself will give you a sign: The virgin will conceive and give birth to a son, and will call him Immanuel" (Isaiah 7:14).

Mary, naturally, was confused. "How can that happen if I'm a virgin?"

Gabriel told her the Holy Spirit would make it happen, and that even her cousin Elizabeth was miraculously pregnant.

Mary humbly agreed to whatever the Lord had planned.

Her future husband, Joseph, obviously had some questions. He considered breaking off the wedding, but an angel visited him in a dream and told him that God was behind all of it. He agreed to go ahead with their plans.

Later, Mary visited Elizabeth, who was visibly pregnant. When they met, John jumped in Elizabeth's belly, now so near to Jesus who was developing inside Mary. Everyone knew something special was happening here.

His Name Is John (LUKE 1:57–80)

Mary stayed for three months, probably to witness the birth of Elizabeth's baby. Eight days later, according to Jewish rules, Zechariah and Elizabeth took their male baby to the temple to dedicate him to God and receive a name.

Many people threw out suggestions for a name. Zechariah grabbed a writing tablet and wrote, "His name is John!" At that moment, his tongue was released and he spoke. Everyone was amazed.

John grew strong in spirit and lived in the wilderness.

Away in a Manger (LUKE 2:1-40)

At this time, Israel was ruled by the Roman empire, which came after the Persians and Greeks (all of which was prophesied by Daniel!). Around 6 BC, the Roman government held a census—a time of counting all the people so Rome could tax them and get money. Everyone had to register in the town of their family. Joseph, from the line of David, had to get back to his hometown of Bethlehem. But he and Mary arrived too late; all the guest rooms were taken. Someone offered them a place where the animals slept. At least it would be out of the cold.

Prophecy fulfilled:

"But you, Bethlehem Ephrathah,
   though you are small among the
   clans of Judah,
out of you will come for me
   one who will be ruler over Israel,
whose origins are from of old,
   from ancient times" (Micah 5:2).

That night, she gave birth to a boy. There was no crib around, so they placed him in a manger—a feeding trough that animals ate out of.

Nearby, shepherds watched over the fields at night. Suddenly, a whole army of angels appeared in the sky, singing praises to God. "Good news, everyone! Today, in David's town, a Savior was born! The Promised One from Scriptures! You'll find a baby wrapped in cloths and lying in a manger."

The shepherds walked into town and found Joseph, Mary, and baby Jesus. They went and told others, glorifying and praising God.

Eight days after Jesus' birth, Jewish rules said the male baby needed to be taken to the temple, named, and later dedicated to the Lord. Mary and Joseph went and met a man named Simeon, who had been told by the Holy Spirit that he would see the Lord's Messiah. He saw the baby Jesus and praised God.

A woman named Anna, who was a widow, spent over sixty years in the temple waiting to see the Christ. She came to them so excited that she got to see the child.

Wise Guys (MATTHEW 2:1-12)

East of Israel—in the area known as Iran/Iraq today—really smart scholars (known as wise men) read over the Jewish Scriptures, most likely left after the exile of the Jews into Babylon. They saw a prophecy about a star that would announce a king born to the Jews. That star lit up an area to the west of them, toward the nation of Israel. They loaded up their camels and journeyed out to visit.

Naturally, they thought the current king, Herod, knew all about the prophecies and the star hovering over Israel. He did not and told the men to investigate and report back to him. Herod didn't want another king to be born in Israel; he secretly wanted to kill the baby!

The prophecy pointed to the town of Bethlehem, so the wise men went that direction, following the star. When they discovered Mary, Joseph, and the little child Jesus, they fell to their knees and worshiped him. They gave the family gifts of gold, frankincense, and myrrh. On their return to Herod, a dream told them not to say anything to him.

But Herod found out and got mad that the wise men ignored him, so he sent his own soldiers out to Bethlehem to kill all male children two years or younger, according to the information the wise men gave him. (Notice how similar this is to what happened in Moses' day when he was born!) Joseph had a dream to take his family and run safely to Egypt.

Jesus: The Early Years (MATTHEW 2:13-23; LUKE 2:41-52)

Joseph and his family were safe in Egypt. Herod had no power over that area. After Herod died in 4 BC, Joseph had another dream that told him to return. This time the family went to Nazareth, back to their hometown.

Jesus grew up very normal. Like any child, he adopted his father's trade—carpentry. He built things like furniture, but also homes.

We know nothing about Jesus' days before the age of twelve, which traditionally for a Jewish boy is the last year of his childhood. Like all good Jewish families, Joseph and Mary took everyone to Jerusalem for the Passover. A big crowd went along, around seventy people. Once the festivities were over, they returned home.

Three days later, Joseph and Mary realized Jesus wasn't with them. They returned back to Jerusalem and, after

looking everywhere, found him in the temple, talking with rabbis and scholars. These teachers were impressed by Jesus' knowledge.

Joseph and Mary pulled him aside and asked how he could wander off like that. Jesus replied, his first spoken words in the Bible: "Didn't you know you could find me in my Father's house?"

Back in Nazareth, Jesus continued to grow up, physically, mentally, spiritually, becoming a man to the age of thirty. He left home to visit an old friend he met once while in his mother's womb: his cousin John.

WHAT'S THE POINT?

▶ Everyone from simple shepherds to smart scholars sought out Jesus and worshiped him. Everyone is invited to find Jesus.

▶ Very little is known about Jesus during his childhood. He was very normal but learned who he was from his parents and his school days at the local synagogue. By the age of twelve, Jesus knew he was the Son of God.

▶ At Christmastime, we celebrate that God came to earth to be with us. The word *Emmanuel* means "God is with us." It's a humbling act of surrender for God to do so much for us by coming to this earth.

14

Operation Jesus Begins

MATTHEW 3-4; MARK 1; LUKE 3-4; JOHN 1-4

 WHO'S WHO

» **Jesus**—all grown up and ready to get to work

» **John the Baptist**—dunking people in the water and preparing them for the Messiah

» **Andrew**—a follower of John about to become an apostle of Jesus

» **Philip**—one of the first to be called to follow Jesus

» **Nathanael**—an apostle who liked to sit under fig trees

» **Nicodemus**—a Pharisee who snuck around at night

» **Samaritan woman**—all was not well with the woman at the well

WHERE ARE WE?

» **Jordan River**—John's giant baptism bath

» **Wilderness**—a desert-like place where animals and angels hang out

» **Cana**—a small town that ran low on wine

» **Jerusalem**—the home of the temple where Jesus shook things up

» **Samaria**—once the capital of northern Israel; still hated by Jews today

 INTERESTING STUFF IN THIS SECTION

» When Satan tempted Jesus, Jesus responded by using Scripture to stop the temptation.

» Jesus quoted Deuteronomy three times when talking to Satan. Satan quoted Psalms, indicating that Satan knows the Bible.

» The city of Samaria was established during the split that occurred between northern and southern Israel and the two leaders Rehoboam and Jeroboam. Samaria was the capital and had built their own temple because the Jews wouldn't let them worship in Jerusalem. The Samaritans had a strong expectation for a Messiah who would be a prophet like Moses and a revealer of all things.

» John 3:16 is one of the most searched Bible verses ever on the internet.

Hey, Everyone, John's Here (MATTHEW 3:1-7;
MARK 1:1-11; LUKE 3:1-23)

Thirty years later, John grew up and lived in the wilderness down by the Jordan River. (Remember when the Israelites first crossed the Jordan to claim the Promised Land?) He began baptizing people in the river. To be baptized, a person had to make a commitment to be clean of sins, then wash themselves in water to show others that they were forgiven or that their sins were washed away.

John acted as a messenger, telling everyone that the Messiah, the Promised One

> Prophecy fulfilled: "And he will go on before the Lord, in the spirit and power of Elijah, to turn the hearts of the parents to their children and the disobedient to the wisdom of the righteous—to make ready a people prepared for the Lord" (Luke 1:17).

from the Old Testament prophecies, was coming to be with them soon. John wanted everyone to be ready for this Messiah, so they confessed their sins to be cleansed of their sins. People came out to hear John and were baptized; that's why he's known as John the Baptist or Baptizer.

One day, Jesus walked up while John baptized people. John saw him and said, "It's the Lamb of God who has come to take away the sin of the world!" That told people Jesus came as a sacrifice to die for their sins.

Jesus asked to be baptized, then stepped into the water. While John baptized him, a voice came from the skies that

said, "This is my Son and I'm very pleased with him." Then something that looked like a dove descended on Jesus' head. It was the Holy Spirit.

In a rare moment, the entire Trinity (Father, Son, and Holy Spirit) appeared together.

Temptation in the Desert (MATTHEW 4:1-11; MARK 1:12-13; LUKE 4:1-13)

Jesus went into the wilderness and fasted for forty days. That's a long time to go without food, but Jesus wanted to focus on the work that was ahead of him. He removed himself from all distractions and went to a deserted area where no one lived.

> The Israelites walked the wilderness for forty years because of their sin, many times grumbling about their food options. Jesus survived forty days in the wilderness without food and without sinning.

Satan, the devil, thought this would be a great time to tempt Jesus. Jesus was God in a human body. He came to die as a perfect sacrifice, and a perfect sacrifice did not sin. If Jesus listened to Satan's temptations to sin, then Jesus would no longer be worthy to die for our sins.

Satan stood before a hungry Jesus, then told him to turn the rocks around him into bread. Jesus told him a person doesn't live on bread alone. People need spiritual things more than food.

Then Satan took him to Jerusalem and the top of the temple, telling Jesus to throw himself down and let angels catch him. Jesus refused. Satan took him to a high mountain and showed him all the cities, promising Jesus would be the ruler over all of them if he would worship Satan. Jesus refused. He was already God, ruler over everything, and didn't want to rule over a world that was corrupted by sin.

Satan always wanted to be God, so if he could tell God what to do, then he would be greater than God. Jesus shut him down.

Jesus won the test of three temptations. Angels came to him and helped him get his strength back.

Jesus' Students (JOHN 1:35-51)

In those days, a rabbi, or teacher, would ask students to follow him. Jesus wanted to get together a group of twelve men to learn from him over the next three years. These students were known as apostles because Jesus specifically asked them to follow him. Jesus had many disciples but only twelve apostles.

While Jesus walked along, two people followed him. They knew him from the incident with John the Baptist, saying, "There's the Lamb of God!" They stayed and talked with Jesus. One was Andrew, a fisherman from Capernaum. He went home to tell his brother, Simon, that they met the Messiah. They would all meet later.

Jesus came across a man named Philip and said, "Follow me." Philip told his friend Nathanael, "We found the Messiah that the Scriptures promised would come one day. His name is Jesus and he's from Nazareth." Nathanael made a face. "Nazareth? Can anything good come from there?" Philip told him to come meet Jesus.

Jesus saw Nathanael walking up and said, "I saw you while you were sitting under that fig tree." Nathanael wondered, *How did anyone see me back then? I was by myself. Could this be . . . God?*

Nathanael believed. Jesus promised to show him many more incredible things.

Wedding Crashers (JOHN 2:1–12)

Jesus and his followers went to a wedding in Cana, a small town in Galilee. His mom was there. Wedding parties lasted for days back then. The family needed to provide food and drink the entire time, but sadly this wedding ran out of wine very early on. For the host of this party, that was a huge embarrassment.

Jesus' mom, Mary, who was obviously close to the family, went up to Jesus and asked for help. Jesus wondered why she involved him in this problem, but she turned to the servants and told them to follow his lead.

> Wine takes anywhere between two to ten weeks to make. Good wine can take one month and up to five years. Jesus created the best wine the servant ever tasted in just seconds.

Jesus had six huge stone jars filled with water (holding twenty to thirty gallons each). The abundance of wine symbolized the coming of the kingdom and the infinite supply of grace. He then told them to taste the water. It was the best wine they had ever tasted.

Cleanup on Aisle 1 (JOHN 2:13–25)

Passover brought many people to Jerusalem to worship God and follow the law. Jesus also went at the beginning of his ministry.

People were required to bring a sacrifice, such as a cow, sheep, or doves. Many came from all over the world and needed their money changed into the local currency so they could buy those items.

Jesus entered the temple courts and saw chaos where normally people worshiped. They were buying and selling sacrifices, exchanging money, and creating so much noise people couldn't focus

> Prophecy fulfilled: "For zeal for your house consumes me, and the insults of those who insult you fall on me" (Psalm 69:9).

on worship. They were taking advantage of people and getting rich off the things of God. Jesus made a whip and crashed into the tables, tipping them over and telling everyone to stop all this noise!

"You've turned my Father's house into a marketplace!" Jesus loved the temple and what it represented, but people abused it. Later, Jesus returned to this temple and saw that nobody had listened to what he said or made any changes.

How Can You Be "Born Again"? (JOHN 3:1–21)

There were a number of religious leaders during the time of Jesus.

The Pharisees enforced the do's and don'ts of the Jewish faith. They even created their list of additional laws that people could or could not do.

The scribes were like the legal experts, or lawyers, of the law.

The rabbis taught the law, like professors at a college.

The Sadducees believed in the law and humanity, but in nothing spiritual outside what they could see.

However, they all agreed on one thing: Jesus was a threat to them and their jobs. They hated him.

A group of about seventy men who made important religious decisions for Israel was called the Sanhedrin. It was made up of Pharisees, scribes, rabbis, Sadducees, and others who were rich or influential.

Not all of them disagreed with Jesus. A few actually understood his message and accepted him as God and the Messiah. One such person was Nicodemus, a Pharisee. He came to Jesus late one night, when nobody could see him, and asked Jesus how he could perform such signs if God was not with him.

Jesus replied, "Only someone born again can see the kingdom of God."

Nicodemus asked, "How can someone be born again like a baby when they are old?"

Jesus answered, "No, you were born the first time by flesh into the world. This time you have to be born of the Spirit. If you believe by faith, you will have eternal life in you."

> You don't choose to be born the first time, but you do choose to be born the second time, this time by spirit, into a new family—God's.

Then, in John 3:16, we find the most well-known verse in the Bible: "For God so loved the world that he gave his one and only Son, that whoever believes in him shall not perish but have eternal life."

Jesus came to save the world, and if you believe in him, you will be saved.

This is a dark world, overcome by sin. Jesus is the light that shines to expose our sin, so we can confess our sins and live in the light, not in the darkness.

John Under Arrest (MATTHEW 4:12; MARK 1:14; LUKE 3:19-20)

John the Baptist continued to do great things in the wilderness, baptizing people and pointing them to Jesus, saying the Messiah had finally come to earth.

He also spoke truth about sin he saw happening. One person he spoke out against was Herod Antipas. Herod Antipas was the son of Herod the Great, the man who tried to kill the baby Jesus after talking to the wise men. Herod Antipas had a marriage that was against Jewish law, and John told everyone it was wrong.

Herod Antipas had John arrested and put in prison, hoping to silence him. This saddened many of John's followers.

Woman at the Well (JOHN 4:1-42)

Jesus took a trip through an area most Jews avoided— Samaria. The Jews still hated Samaria from nine hundred years ago, when the civil war started. The people in Samaria were part Jewish and not fully committed to the temple and its purposes. For that reason, Jews in southern Jerusalem walked around Samaria to get to Galilee in the north.

Jesus brought his followers to a town named Sychar, specifically to a well in an area Jacob gave Joseph way

back. It was about noon and Jesus rested at the well while his followers went into town to get some food.

A Samaritan woman came to get water, a task most people did in the cool morning, because dragging water so far in the heat of the day was hard. Jesus asked her for a drink. That was unusual because Jews didn't talk to Samaritans, and men didn't talk to women when alone with them.

When she asked why, he said, "I have water that is living. When you drink this water, you'll never be thirsty again. In fact, it will give you eternal life."

"Sir, give me this water so I don't have to keep coming back."

Jesus said to go call her husband. She shook her head. She didn't have a husband. Then Jesus said, "You're correct, you've had five husbands and the man you are with now isn't your husband."

The Samaritan woman immediately knew he was a prophet. "I know the Messiah is coming, and when he does, he will explain everything we need to know."

Jesus said, "I am he." The woman ran into town and told everyone what happened. Many Samaritans believed the

> This water is called "living water" because it flows like a river, not sitting still like a pond. This living water is seen in heaven in John's book of Revelation:
>
> > "For the Lamb at the center of the throne will be their shepherd; 'he will lead them to springs of living water'" (Revelation 7:17).

woman and asked Jesus to stay a few days. Many more became true believers.

The excitement surrounding Jesus was building and many miracles were to come, especially in an area called Galilee.

WHAT'S THE POINT?

▸ The people of Jesus' day practiced their religion according to the rules. They followed the laws—do this, don't do that—and went to all the festivals, like Passover. Jesus tried to show them that the relationship with God was by faith, according to their love for God, not because they had to. Believers today should follow Jesus and his teachings rather than laws.

▸ While people like the Pharisees had a hard time with Jesus, Samaritans did not. It proves that education doesn't make you smart, but humility and faith do.

▸ Jesus still calls people to follow him even though he isn't here physically on the earth. We can follow his words and still do what he asks us to do today.

▸ Jesus went to people that his own people didn't like. Sometimes God may ask us to be friends with an unpopular crowd.

15

Miracles 'R' Jesus

MATTHEW 4–18; MARK 1–9; LUKE 4–9; JOHN 4–6

WHO'S WHO

» **Jesus**—the miracle maker

» **Peter**—the (temporary) water walker

» **Matthew**—a tax collector

» **Andrew**—Peter's bro

WHERE ARE WE?

» **Galilee**—a region in northern Israel where lots of fishermen hung out

» **Capernaum**—Jesus' new hometown

» **Nazareth**—Jesus' old hometown

» **Cana**—where Jesus crashed a wedding

» **Gadarenes or Gerasenes**—where some really wild people lived

INTERESTING STUFF IN THIS SECTION

» Jesus multiplied food just like Elijah and Elisha did in smaller quantities with olive oil and flour. Jesus healed people from leprosy just like Elijah did. Even Elijah and Elisha brought people back to life. But Jesus did it more often, in larger numbers, and in a variety of ways.

» Jesus walked across water in a better way than Moses could by splitting the sea.

» Elisha prayed for a drought, but Jesus told a storm to stop immediately. He showed his power over nature that had been damaged by sin in anticipation of when all creation will be restored.

» Jesus healed people who were close or far away.

Thumbs Up and Thumbs Down (MATTHEW 4:13-22; MARK 1:14-20; LUKE 4:14-30; JOHN 4:43-54)

Galilee was a region north of Jerusalem and Samaria, surrounding the Sea of Galilee. The area was mostly Jewish. The people there survived off livestock and farm animals, agriculture, and fishing around the large body of water known as the Sea of Galilee.

When Jesus started his ministry there, many people listened and believed. Galilee would be where Jesus did most of his work, traveling occasionally south to Jerusalem for the Jewish festivals. In many parts of Galilee, they welcomed Jesus.

Once, while in Cana (where he turned the water to wine), Jesus met a royal official from Capernaum whose son was very close to death. The man traveled miles to beg Jesus to heal his son. Jesus simply said, "Your son will live." As the man returned home, a servant ran to him, saying his son was alive and feeling better. When they figured out the time the son got healthy, it was exactly when Jesus said those words. The entire household of the royal official believed in Jesus.

Jesus traveled to his hometown in Nazareth, but he did not get a warm welcome there. On the Sabbath, he entered the local synagogue and read from the prophet Isaiah.

> "The Spirit of the Sovereign LORD is on me,
>> because the LORD has anointed me
>> to proclaim good news to the poor.
> He has sent me to bind up the brokenhearted,
>> To proclaim freedom for the captives
> and release from darkness for the prisoners,
>> to proclaim the year of the LORD's favor" (Isaiah
>> 61:1–2).

He turned to the people and said, "Today this has been fulfilled." The people knew he meant that he fulfilled the prophecy as the promised Messiah, but they remembered him only as the little boy growing up with Joseph and Mary. Jesus knew no prophet could be accepted in his hometown. The people tried to throw him off a cliff for claiming to be God, but Jesus slipped away.

Jesus walked along the shore of the Sea of Galilee and saw two brothers fishing—Simon (also known as Peter) and Andrew. They were not having a good day fishing, their nets coming up empty. They called it a day, but Jesus came up and told them to put their nets down in the deep water. Peter and Andrew did, and their nets filled with so many fish the nets overflowed. Two other fishermen brothers came to help them— James and John, sons of Zebedee.

> Fishing for fish and fishing for people both require patience, knowing the proper bait, and knowing the right time to catch them.

Jesus asked all four of them to follow him, saying they would fish for people now. Peter, Andrew, James, and John left their fishing business to follow Jesus.

So Many Miracles (MATTHEW 4:13-25; 8:2-4; 9:2-17; MARK 1:14-2:22; LUKE 4:31-5:39)

Capernaum was a town in Galilee, right along the sea, where many fishermen lived. It was a Jewish city and had a synagogue, where Jesus taught on a Sabbath. People loved him, except for a man possessed by a demon, who told Jesus to go away. "I know who you are," the demon said. "The holy one of God." Jesus told the demon to get out of the man and it did. The people couldn't believe what they just saw.

At Simon Peter's house, Jesus found out Peter's mother-in-law had a fever. Jesus told the fever to go away and it did. She stood up and started serving the others. By sunset, many more people brought the sick and demon-possessed to him, and Jesus healed all of them.

Word started to spread all over about Jesus' power and ability. As the crowds grew and grew, Jesus needed to get away by himself at times and pray.

A man with leprosy fell on the ground before Jesus and asked if Jesus was willing to cleanse him of this sickness. Jesus said he was willing, and the leprosy went away.

While Jesus relaxed in a home in Capernaum, a crowd surrounded the house, making it difficult for anyone to get close. Four men carried their paralyzed friend on a mat so Jesus could heal him. Unable to get close, they climbed up on the roof, punched through, and lowered the friend down to Jesus. Jesus loved their faith.

When someone had leprosy, they had to be quarantined and kept from others so they would not spread the highly contagious and deadly disease through the air.

Jesus saw that a few Pharisees and teachers of law were watching. So Jesus told the man, "Your sins are forgiven." They wondered how someone could forgive all of a person's sins. Jesus turned to the religious leaders and asked, "Which is easier—to forgive this man's sins or tell him to get up and walk?" Trick question—both of these were things only God could do.

Then Jesus told the man to pick up his mat and walk away. The man did. Everyone praised God, except those Pharisees and teachers.

The Romans hired local Jewish men to collect the taxes. It was not a popular job, but it paid well because the tax collector could overcharge and keep the difference. A tax collector could make good money but lose all his friends.

Jesus walked by a tax collector's booth where a man named Levi sat. Levi was also known as Matthew. Jesus asked Matthew to follow him and join the other apostles. Matthew quit his job as a tax collector and joined Jesus. This had to make the others uncomfortable.

Matthew was so excited about this new adventure, he threw a huge party and invited his friends to meet Jesus. They did, while the Pharisees watched, unable to believe that a good teacher like Jesus would eat with all these tax collectors and sinners. Jesus told them, "It's the sick who need a doctor, not those who think they are well."

Paralysis, Demons, and Death? No Problem!
(MATTHEW 12; MARK 2:23–3:19; LUKE 6:1–19; JOHN 5)

The Jews went to Jerusalem routinely to celebrate a number of festivals that started with Moses. Those holy days included the Feast of the Tabernacles (or Tents), Day of Atonement, Pentecost, and Passover. The temple in Jerusalem was the only place where a priest could perform a sacrifice.

Once, while Jesus was in Jerusalem, he saw a paralyzed man by a pool of water in Bethesda. Many believed that when the water stirred, an angel was nearby, so everyone dove into the pool. The paralyzed man could never get there in time. Jesus asked the man, "Do you want to get well?" The man did. Jesus told him to stand up and walk. The man did.

The Jewish leaders in town heard about this and asked the man how someone could heal on the Sabbath and break the law. The man didn't care. He could walk!

Jesus later healed another man on the Sabbath, in Capernaum at the synagogue. The Jewish leaders asked Jesus if healing on the Sabbath was against the law.

> The fourth commandment says, "Remember the Sabbath day by keeping it holy. Six days you shall labor and do all your work, but the seventh day is a sabbath to the LORD your God. On it you shall not do any work, neither you, nor your son or daughter, nor your male or female servant, nor your animals, nor any foreigner residing in your towns." For Pharisees, "work" meant healing someone from a crippling disease.

Jesus said if they were okay to help a sheep that fell into a pit on the Sabbath, why not assist a person who needs help?

To prove his point, Jesus saw a man with a shriveled (not fully grown) hand. He told the man to stretch it out, and it was restored. People freaked out, especially the

Pharisees who wanted to kill Jesus, because now everyone liked him.

Super Sermon (MATTHEW 5-8; LUKE 6:20-49)

By this point, Jesus had all twelve apostles. They were Simon (Peter), Andrew (Peter's brother), James and John (also brothers), Philip, Nathanael (also known as Bartholomew), Matthew the former tax collector, Thomas (who had a twin), James (known as the *lesser*, which means younger or small), another Simon who was called the Zealot, Judas the son of James, and Judas Iscariot, who will betray Jesus later.

Near the shores of Bethsaida, a large crowd followed Jesus. He found a place to sit, like a rabbi would when he was about to speak. The people stopped to listen. There on an incline, or mount, Jesus began to teach a lengthy sermon that covered many topics, providing new light on old ways of thinking.

He taught about what really, really pleases God. He listed things such as *poor in spirit, mourning, persecuted,* or *weak.* Jesus said Christians are like salt, preserving truth on this earth and adding flavoring to a dull world. Christians are also light, shining in a dark world.

> Moses gave the law from Mount Sinai. Jesus gave a new law from a hillside in Bethsaida. Jesus' purpose was to show a new way to look at the law.

Jesus showed them that sin does not only happen physically (such as murder or sex outside of marriage), but mentally. People should also keep their promises. He spoke about equal and fair justice for crimes.

Then he told people to love their enemies and go the extra mile for them. Jesus taught how to give properly and how to pray, providing a nice outline for prayer. Jesus talked about those trying to get rich in this world and serving two masters—God and money. It's impossible. A person must choose one or the other.

Jesus comforted people, telling them not to worry because God knows their needs and provides. Finally, he wrapped up by saying that his followers cannot judge people, and encouraged them to ask God, seek his will, and find fulfillment through him.

Doubts and Faith (MATTHEW 8:5–13:13; MARK 3:20–22; 4:1–34; LUKE 7:1–8:18)

From there, Jesus traveled back to Capernaum, where messengers from a Roman centurion met him. A centurion was a ruler in the Roman army; they usually didn't get along with the Israelites. But this centurion was loved by many because he loved Israel and gave money to the local synagogue. The centurion had a servant who got very sick, and wanted Jesus' help. He knew Jesus had authority, just like the centurion had authority to tell people to go here and do this or that. The centurion felt Jesus didn't even need to come to the house; he could just say the word and the servant would be healed. Jesus admired his faith, trusting in God's authority. The servant was healed when the messengers returned to their home.

Later, they all traveled to a small town called Nain, where they saw a funeral procession carrying the body of the only son of a poor widow. Jesus touched the stretcher that carried the body, and the son sat up and began to talk. Everyone praised God.

Meanwhile, as John the Baptist sat in prison, he began to express doubts, wondering if Jesus was really the Promised One John told everyone he was. John sent messengers to Jesus to ask that question. Jesus reaffirmed that many diseases and sicknesses were healed, sight was given to the blind, and demons were cast out of people. So yes, it was definitely Jesus who fulfilled all that was required by the Messiah.

A Pharisee invited Jesus over for dinner. While Jesus reclined at the table, a sinful woman stopped by and poured perfume on his feet, sobbing and wiping his feet with her hair. The Pharisee could not believe Jesus would allow a woman with such a bad reputation to touch him. Jesus said those who have been forgiven more show more emotion. He forgave her of all her sins. The others at the table wondered, *Who is this guy who forgives sins?*

Once, they brought a demon-possessed man to Jesus. The demon caused blindness and deafness in the man. The Pharisees accused Jesus of being the prince of all demons, since he could command demons out of people. Jesus said their charge was ridiculous. "No kingdom attacks its own kingdom, so why would demons cast out demons?" said Jesus.

Jesus frequently spoke in parables to help people understand his teachings. Parables are stories that have a spiritual meaning. One parable talked about seeds on different types of soil. The seeds represented faith and the soil represented people's hearts. Depending on the soil, faith cannot grow unless the heart is good and welcomes God.

> **Prophecy fulfilled:**
>
> "I will open my mouth with a parable; I will utter hidden things, things from of old" (Psalm 78:2).
>
> "Son of man, set forth an allegory and tell it to the Israelites as a parable" (Ezekiel 17:2).

Jesus mainly taught about the kingdom of heaven, using parables about weeds, mustard seeds, yeast used to make bread rise, a treasure hidden in a field, and a net tossed out to catch many fish. He wanted his followers to understand that God's kingdom needed to grow on earth. While some would accept this truth, many would reject it.

Be Quiet, Storms and Demons! (MATTHEW 8-9; MARK 4-5; LUKE 8)

Jesus got into a boat with his disciples and they sailed across the Sea of Galilee. While Jesus napped on a cushion, a terrible storm rocked the boat. The disciples screamed for help! Jesus calmly woke up and asked them why they had so little faith. He told the storm to be quiet and it did.

> According to Roman army standards, a legion equaled between three thousand and six thousand. Hard to imagine that many demons in one man.

They arrived on the opposite shore of the sea and were met by a wild madman. He was demon-possessed and lived in the cemetery, violently breaking any chains used to hold him down. When the man saw Jesus, he ran to him, shouting, "What do you want with us? Why are you here to torture us?" Jesus asked the demon his name. "We are Legion, because there are many of us in here."

The demons knew their time was short, so they asked Jesus to throw them into a herd of pigs. Jesus did and the pigs ran into the sea to drown. The man, now healed, sat dazed on the ground. He asked Jesus if he could join the other disciples, but Jesus told him to instead go back to his hometown and show everyone what God could do.

Traveling to Nazareth, Jesus faced more rejection from his own people. "Isn't this the son of Joseph the carpenter? Isn't his mom Mary and his brothers James, Joseph, Simon, and Judas? We know his sisters, too. Who does he think he is?" Jesus shook his head. "A prophet gets no honor in his hometown." He didn't do any miracles there because they didn't believe.

On the other hand, Jesus and his followers entered Capernaum to a huge welcome. People lined the streets cheering for him, pressing in on him closer and closer. A leader from the synagogue named Jairus pushed through, falling at Jesus' feet. He begged Jesus to come heal his only daughter, twelve years old, who was dying.

While Jesus walked through the crowd to get to Jairus' house, a woman who had been bleeding internally for twelve years tried to get close to Jesus. Many doctors had tried to help her, but nothing worked. She reached out and could only touch his cloak. Immediately, her bleeding stopped.

Jesus felt his power leave his body and asked who touched him. The woman, afraid, confessed. Jesus, impressed by her faith, told her that her faith healed her. Right then, someone ran up to Jairus and said, "Your daughter is dead." Jesus comforted him, telling him not to be afraid—just believe.

As Jesus arrived at the house, people mourned and played sad music. Jesus told them to stop crying. "The girl is not dead. She's only asleep." The sad crowd broke into laughter, finding Jesus' response silly. Jesus touched the little girl's hand and told her to stand up. She did. No one laughed at Jesus then.

Prophecy fulfilled: "In that day the deaf will hear the words of the scroll, and out of gloom and darkness the eyes of the blind will see" (Isaiah 29:18).

From there, Jesus saw two blind men who cried out for mercy. Jesus touched their eyes and their eyesight came back. Then a demon-possessed man who could not talk was brought to Jesus. Jesus drove the demon out and the man could speak.

Multiplying Miracles (MATTHEW 13:54–14:36; MARK 6; LUKE 9:1–17; JOHN 6)

Knowing that he had taught his apostles well, Jesus sent them out in twos with the power to drive out demons from people and cure any diseases they faced. He told them to pack lightly, trusting God to provide, and to proclaim the good news everywhere they went. They did so, returning with incredible stories about what they saw and did.

On Herod's birthday, the daughter of his wife performed a dance that Herod really liked, so he asked her what she wanted and he would give her anything. The girl went to her mother, Herodias, who told her to ask for

John the Baptist's head on a platter. Since the king said he would give her anything she wanted, he had to do it. John was beheaded and his head brought to Herod on a platter. John's disciples buried his body, then told Jesus what had happened.

In a remote area near Bethsaida, a huge crowd of five thousand men, plus thousands of women and children, followed Jesus and listened to him speak about the kingdom of God. It was late in the afternoon. Jesus knew none of them had eaten, so he turned to his apostles and asked how they would feed all these people. Calculating the food costs, they knew it would cost half a year's wages to feed all these people. They decided the best answer was to send them into the village to buy food. Jesus didn't like that answer. He told them to feed the people.

Philip found a boy with five loaves of bread and two fish. That was the best they could do. Jesus told everyone to sit down in groups of fifty to one hundred. Then he took the five loaves, looked to heaven, and gave thanks. As he broke the bread, more and more bread appeared. Basketfuls after basketfuls. It was distributed to the people. The same amazing multiplication happened with the fish. Thousands and thousands out of nowhere.

Everyone ate and was satisfied. There were even leftovers—one basketful for each of the twelve apostles. They could have started a fish-and-chips business.

After the miracle, Jesus told the disciples to get into the boat as he dismissed the crowd. As they set sail over the sea, Jesus went off to pray on land. Later that night, the boat was far offshore, but the waves and wind kept it from moving forward. They were stuck. As the disciples rowed, they looked up, and there was Jesus walking on water. They were terrified, thinking he was a ghost. Jesus told them not to be afraid.

Peter said, "Well, if it is you, ask me to join you on the water."

Jesus agreed. Peter stepped out of the boat and also walked on water, then he took his eyes off Jesus and saw

the wind and waves. Peter panicked and sank, calling out for help. Jesus caught him. "You have so little faith. Why did you doubt?" They got to the other side—Capernaum—and Jesus healed many people there.

At the synagogue in Capernaum, a number of religious leaders cornered Jesus with questions. They had seen the feeding of the five thousand plus, even eaten the bread Jesus multiplied, but they wanted to trap him with questions. Jesus talked about bread, saying God brought bread down from heaven to earth so Moses and the Israelites could eat. That kind of heavenly bread gives life to the world.

The accusers asked for this bread. Jesus replied, "I am the bread of life that has come down from heaven. If you believe in me, you will never go hungry." The Jewish religious leaders grumbled. How could Jesus come from heaven? They knew Joseph, his father. Jesus corrected them, saying his Father was in heaven and sent him to draw people closer to God.

> "He humbled you, causing you to hunger and then feeding you with manna, which neither you nor your ancestors had known, to teach you that man does not live on bread alone but on every word that comes from the mouth of the LORD" (Deuteronomy 8:3).

This did not sit well with his accusers. Not even with some of his disciples, who turned away from him. Jesus turned to the twelve and asked them if they wanted to leave. Peter said, "Where would we go? You have words of eternal life. We believe you are the holy one of God."

Road Trip (MATTHEW 15-16; MARK 7-8; LUKE 9:18-27)

Jewish leaders came up to Galilee from Jerusalem to destroy Jesus' credibility. They loved to attack how Jesus and his disciples never kept the Jewish laws, such as washing their hands before they ate. Jesus told them that it's not what goes into a person's mouth that defiles their soul; it's what comes out of their heart (lying, hate, evil) that makes them sinful. He called the Pharisees and others blind guides who lead the blind and fall into pits.

Jesus took his followers north of Galilee, on a road trip, to an area known as Tyre and Sidon. He ministered to a number of people there who were not followers of the Jewish customs but had some Jewish blood in them. Remember, the Jews did not associate with these people and called them Gentiles.

In this area, he met a Canaanite woman who cried out for help because her daughter was possessed by a demon. Jesus told her that he came only for the lost people from Israel. She replied, "But even those of us who aren't Jewish will take whatever crumbs of hope that fall from your table." Jesus loved that answer, and immediately her daughter was healed.

Jesus walked a little farther to a region known as the Decapolis. The people brought a deaf man who could barely speak. Jesus took him aside, put his fingers in the man's ears, then spit and touched the man's tongue. He cried, "Be opened!" and the man's ears opened up. The people went wild!

Huge crowds began to follow Jesus, bringing the blind, crippled, mute, and many others. Jesus healed everyone he could. His heart broke for them since many had followed him for three days. Jesus wanted to feed them, so he asked the disciples how they could feed the four thousand men in front of them.

The disciples returned to the same answer they gave before at the feeding of the five thousand. "We don't have enough money or bread." Jesus asked how many loaves they had. They could only find seven loaves and a few small fish.

Once again, just like before, the people sat in groups and Jesus gave thanks for the bread and fish in his hands. Then Jesus multiplied food over and over, more and more, filling basket after basket, feeding the four thousand men plus women and children. The people ate and were satisfied. There were even seven baskets left over.

> Why did the apostles not remember the feeding of the five thousand? Probably because these were not Jews, and certainly Jesus wasn't going to feed them too? But Jesus did, showing that he loved all people equally.

Jesus and his disciples got into a boat and sailed away.

The Pharisees demanded a sign from Jesus that he was the one who all those Old Testament prophecies pointed to. Jesus told them to look to the sign of Jonah—the prophet swallowed by a fish and who lived for three days in the fish's stomach before the fish spit him out alive on dry ground. That's the same sign they would all soon see. Jesus was, of course, talking about his death and spending three days in a grave, after which he would step out of the grave, alive and resurrected.

Jesus took his disciples on another road trip, this time to Caesarea Philippi. The area was known for its worship of idols like Zeus, Pan, and other Roman gods. He sat them all down and asked, "Who do people say I am?"

The disciples said a number of things. "Some think you're John the Baptist come back from the dead, or Elijah the prophet from long ago. Some even say Jeremiah."

Jesus listened, then asked, "But who do you say that I am?"

Peter spoke up. "You are the Messiah, the son of the living God."

Jesus lit up. "That's right, Peter, and on that truth, I'm going to build my church, and the gates of hell and death won't be able to stop it!" Jesus went on to explain that he would be put into the hands of the chief priests, then be killed, but three days later he would come back to life. Peter tried to stop him from talking such nonsense, but Jesus said only Satan could make Peter say that.

> This is the first time the word *church* is used in the Bible.

Jesus then spoke very plainly and clearly. "Look, if you want to follow me, you'll have to deny yourself, take up a cross, and go with me to death. If you try to save your life, you'll lose your life. But if you are willing to lose your life for me, you'll gain it. You can gain this whole world but lose your soul. Don't do it."

Jesus Is the Greatest (MATTHEW 17–18; MARK 9; LUKE 9:18–62)

In the northern part of Israel, Jesus took Peter, James, and John up a mountain. He stood before them and was transfigured or transformed, revealing his godly self that was clothed in a human body. His face shone like the sun; his clothes were as white as light. Next to him, on each side, stood Moses and Elijah.

As Peter, James, and John watched in shock, a voice from heaven said, "This is my Son, whom I love. I'm very pleased with him, so listen to what he says." The three men fell on their faces, but when they looked up, only Jesus stood before them.

> This is the second time God spoke from heaven to confirm Jesus was his son. God even said two times he was pleased with him.

Later, as they left the mountain and a crowd gathered around them, a man knelt before Jesus, pleading for Jesus to show mercy to his son. The son had a demon that threw him into seizures, tossing him one moment into the fire, the next into water. The disciples couldn't heal him. Jesus yelled at the demon, and the demon left the boy.

The disciples wondered why they couldn't heal the boy. Jesus said to them, "Because you have so little faith. You only need faith the size of a mustard seed to tell mountain-sized problems to go from here to there. If you have faith, nothing will be impossible for you."

Jesus and his followers entered Capernaum, and the temple tax collectors found him. The temple tax paid for the upkeep of the temple in Jerusalem and paid the salaries of the priests. They tried to see where Jesus' loyalty was. Jesus told Peter to go fishing and throw out his line. Inside the fish, Jesus predicted, Peter would find a coin to pay the tax. Peter did what he was asked and the fish he caught had the coin inside.

The disciples at times got conceited, feeling they were better than others because they got to hang out with Jesus. Jesus told them that the great people in God's kingdom came to God like humble children, with childlike faith.

The best people in God's kingdom serve others because Jesus is the greatest, even though he himself served others.

He warned them not to cause other people to stumble in their lives, especially little children. Jesus promised a very severe punishment for people like that.

Jesus told them to pray according to God's will; it's the type of prayer that always gets an answer.

He said his followers must forgive those who sin against them. How many times? Like, seven? No, Jesus answered, seven times seventy-seven times. Like, all the time. People who know they have been forgiven of such a huge debt should easily forgive others who have hurt them.

Following Jesus, he emphasized, is not easy. There's hardship and persecution. A person has to leave behind this world and focus on heaven.

But it's worth it.

WHAT'S THE POINT?

► Jesus had to do miracles to show the people that he was God. Only God could do miracles like this. Jesus didn't want to do miracles for the Pharisees, who wanted to boss Jesus around (like Satan at the temptations).

► Jesus healed in many different ways; he wanted to show us that he can heal in any way he wants. There's no formula.

- ▶ Jesus was the lead creator of the earth. Only the creator could walk on water, quiet storms, and fix bodies.

- ▶ Jesus' miracles look forward to a time when he will fix everything—people and nature.

16

Jerusalem, Jericho, and Judea

LUKE 10, 17–19; JOHN 7–11

WHO'S WHO

» **Jesus**—making friends with short guys and dead guys

» **Zacchaeus**—a little guy who hates big crowds

» **Mary and Martha**—Lazarus' sisters, who will never doubt Jesus again

» **Lazarus**—one of two people who walked out of a tomb

WHERE ARE WE?

» **Jericho**—famous for its fallen walls

» **Jerusalem**—the big city with a big problem

» **Bethany**—Lazarus became its number one tourist attraction

INTERESTING STUFF IN THIS SECTION

» Lazarus beat Jesus' time dead by one day. But Lazarus didn't raise himself from the dead; Jesus had him beat on that one.

» While Jesus was in the south part of Israel, he never visited Bethlehem, where he was born.

» The passage in John 8 featuring the woman caught in adultery does not appear in all the copies of John that have been discovered. It appears someone added it later. However, the story fits so true to what we love about Jesus.

The Big City of Jerusalem (JOHN 7-8)

The Jews in Galilee regularly walked to Jerusalem for specific festivals to celebrate God. Those festivals included the Feast of the Tabernacles, Day of Atonement, Pentecost, and especially Passover. Local synagogues were good for daily and weekly teaching and worship, but the sacrifices could only occur at the temple, where God dwelled, and the priests performed the sacrifices.

Since Jesus was born into a Jewish family, he practiced the Jewish laws and participated in the festivals. For three years, Jesus taught his disciples and walked with them all over Israel. Galilee, the region north of Jerusalem, was where Jesus and the apostles made their home. Many times, they traveled to the southern region of Israel, called Judea, to visit Jerusalem and other cities such as Bethany,

Jericho, and an area called Perea on the other side of the Jordan River.

In Jerusalem, especially during Passover festivals, many crowds gathered, and religious leaders were in full force. When Jesus taught, the common people were very interested and felt welcomed by Jesus. This same teaching, on the other hand, made the religious leaders mad. Jesus talked about the relationship between God and people. The religious leaders always put themselves between God and people and didn't like anyone saying otherwise.

This is why they called Jesus "demon-possessed" and said he was out of his mind. When Jesus healed people on the Sabbath, a no-work day, they said he broke Moses' law. The problem, Jesus told them, was that they didn't know the law. When Jesus talked about how close his relationship was with God the Father, they called him a blasphemer, meaning someone who said bad things against God.

The chief priests tried to have him arrested many times, but he kept getting away. In fact, one time, when Jesus talked about being "living water," the guards who were sent to arrest him returned to the chief priests and Pharisees saying how amazing his teaching was. People like Nicodemus spoke up in defense of Jesus—but talk like that could get you kicked out of the temple, a bad thing for a Jew.

These same religious leaders brought a woman to him who was accused of sleeping with someone outside of marriage. Moses' law said that sin was punishable by death and they could stone her. Jesus, instead, wrote in the sand and said, "Okay, if you're without sin, then throw the first stone." Nobody could claim to be sinless, so they dropped their rocks and left. Jesus told the woman to leave and stop sinning.

Jesus also said things like, "I am the light of the world," which the Pharisees didn't like, wondering who could prove such a claim. Jesus said he had two witnesses—himself, since he was the Son of God, and God, his Father.

In fact, Jesus added that Abraham looked forward to this day when Jesus would walk the earth. They laughed because Jesus was barely thirty years old, and Abraham was alive almost two thousand years before them. Jesus replied, "Before Abraham was alive, I existed."

The Pharisees exploded with anger because Jesus was making himself equal to God. Jesus called them self-righteous, thinking they were right according to their own laws. This made the religious leaders more and more convinced that Jesus needed to die. They wanted to stone him, but again, Jesus escaped. It was not his time to die. Not yet.

Blind Men See (LUKE 10; JOHN 9–10)

Just like Jesus did with sending out the twelve to heal and cast out demons, Jesus did again in the region of Judea, this time with seventy-two of his followers. They returned with wonderful stories of saving people from disease and demons.

Jesus' two greatest commandments are found in the book of Deuteronomy.

Jesus later met up with an expert in religious law. These people knew the Scriptures inside and out, but Jesus knew it better. He asked, "What are the greatest commandments?" When the expert didn't know how to answer, Jesus listed two:

1. Love God with all your heart, soul, strength, and mind.
2. Love your neighbor as much as you love yourself.

The expert asked Jesus to clearly define who was his neighbor. Jesus told a great story of a man who was robbed and beaten and left on the side of the road. Two Jews walked by him, but a Samaritan (whom the Jews didn't like) helped the man back to life. Jesus said that Samaritan treated a stranger like a neighbor.

Jesus and his followers passed a blind man on the side of the road. One of them asked, "Who sinned that caused that man his blindness?" Jesus said that this blind man was blind so that people could see the works of God in Jesus' healing power. Jesus spit in the mud and put it in the blind man's eyes. He told the man to wash his eyes in the Pool of Siloam. When the man did so, he could see.

The Pharisees investigated this incident because the healing happened on the Sabbath. They were upset that Jesus would make mud, because that was work, according to their laws. The Pharisees talked to the blind man's parents and the blind man. All the blind man could say is this: "I don't know if this man was a sinner or not, but I know this—I was blind, but now I see."

Jesus found the man and introduced himself. The man now knew it was Jesus who healed him. Jesus confronted the Pharisees, saying they were the real blind ones because they couldn't see their sin or God standing right in front of them. This made them madder.

It was commonly but incorrectly believed that those who were sick, blind, deaf, or paralyzed were being punished for their sin or the sin of their parents.

Jesus used a lot of descriptions of himself so we could understand him better. In the Old Testament, the prophets called out the "shepherds"—not the people who guided sheep, but the religious leaders who guided people. Jesus called himself "the good shepherd," meaning he was an excellent spiritual leader for people. He called the religious leaders a threat, comparing them to wolves and robbers.

> The Pharisees added 613 more laws to the rules already in the Bible.

As a good shepherd, Jesus promised to lead his sheep to eternal life. He would be willing to sacrifice his life so the sheep could live. Jesus said his sheep knew his voice and no one could snatch them from him because they were given to him by God, his Father. Then Jesus declared, "I and the Father are one." That was a declaration that he was God and he was equal with God.

Once again, the religious leaders picked up stones to kill him. But again, Jesus slipped away.

Dead Men Walk (LUKE 14; JOHN 11)

Jesus and his followers went to Perea on the east side of the Jordan River. It's where John the Baptist first started baptizing people. He was eating at a Pharisee's house when a sick man, swollen with fluid, was brought to him. It was the Sabbath, so Jesus knew what they were thinking. But he healed the man, then said that if the law says it's okay to lift an ox out of a well on the Sabbath, why can't he heal this poor guy?

The crowds followed him, and Jesus told them that there was a price to be his disciple. To be a disciple, one had to understand the love of God. He told three parables about God's love. First, about a shepherd willing to leave ninety-nine sheep to find a single lost sheep. Second, about a homeowner who turned the house upside down to find a lost coin. Finally, about a father waiting for his runaway son and hugging him when he returned.

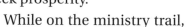

He told them not to lose faith, be humble, and don't seek prosperity.

While on the ministry trail, Jesus received word from Mary and Martha that their brother, Lazarus, was very sick and near death in their hometown of Bethany. Jesus decided not to go right away. He said Lazarus' sickness wouldn't lead to his death but to God's glory. After two days, Jesus directed everyone toward Bethany. When they arrived, Martha ran out and said Jesus was too late. Her brother was dead. . . . If only Jesus had gotten there on time.

Jesus replied, "I am the resurrection and the life. Whoever believes in me will live after they die. I will give them eternal life." Mary, Lazarus' other sister, also arrived. She too wished Jesus had arrived days earlier. When Jesus saw all the crying and sadness around, he too wept. He demanded to go to Lazarus' tomb.

> The Bible passage "Jesus wept" is the shortest verse in the Bible. (John 11:35)

Dead people in those days were wrapped in cloths, then placed in a tomb, and a rock was rolled over the entrance to keep animals and thieves out. Jesus asked the people to roll the stone back that sealed Lazarus' tomb. Everyone thought this was a bad idea because he had been dead for four days. Dead men really stink. But they did it anyway.

Jesus looked into the tomb and yelled, "Lazarus, come out!" Then a man wrapped in cloths stumbled out. They unwrapped him. It was Lazarus, alive and well.

News of this went viral. Everyone talked about it. Many came to see Lazarus. The religious leaders didn't like it. They wanted Jesus dead . . . and Lazarus too. Jesus moved around to smaller towns around Jerusalem.

The Short Guy from Jericho (LUKE 17:11-19; 18:35-19:27)

One of those places was Jericho, the town that Joshua defeated and its walls came crumbling down. As Jesus approached it, ten lepers cried out for Jesus to heal them. He told them to go see the priest and that they would be well. All were healed and nine went on their way, but one—a Samaritan—came back to thank Jesus. Jesus told him that his faith is what really made him well, down to his spirit, because he showed faith and appreciation.

As Jesus continued on, he met a blind beggar who cried out to him for mercy. Jesus asked what he wanted. The man wanted to see. Jesus said, "Your faith has made you well." The man could see!

A large crowd lining the streets greeted Jesus in Jericho. The crowds were so tight, a small man named Zacchaeus tried to see over people's heads. Since he was a chief tax collector, probably nobody helped him or moved aside. So Zacchaeus climbed a sycamore tree. Jesus saw him and liked his effort. Jesus didn't care that Zacchaeus was a hated tax collector; he asked to eat at Zacchaeus's house. Zacchaeus agreed.

Jesus and his disciples enjoyed a nice feast. Zacchaeus, a wealthy man, listened to Jesus talk and immediately wanted to make things right and give back money he took improperly. He promised to sell half his possessions and pay back people with more than he took. Jesus said, "Salvation has come to this house."

Jesus made his way to Jerusalem. The followers got excited, believing Jesus was going to conquer the Romans and take back Israel. Jesus tried to remind them that this was not his kingdom.

Jesus was about to die for the real kingdom.

WHAT'S THE POINT?

▶ Jesus made an effort to go to the people the Jews did not like (e.g., lepers and tax collectors). He needed to show them that God loves everyone; he asks his followers to do the same.

▶ Jesus attacked the religious leaders all the time because they were not leading God's people to God.

▶ Jesus' constant attack of the Pharisees and the Sanhedrin (the Jewish religious court) led them to arrest Jesus and lead him to the cross. They had no idea they were part of the plan to bring salvation to the world.

▶ Jesus stated many "I am's" to define himself as God, the great "I am" who introduced himself to Moses.

17

The Cross

MATTHEW 21-27; MARK 11-15; LUKE 20-23; JOHN 12-19

 WHO'S WHO

» **Jesus**—our Savior, Lord, sacrifice

» **Pilate**—Roman governor whose wife had bad dreams

» **Herod Antipas**—a king who thought he was a king, but he wasn't

» **Caiaphas**—the high priest who thought he was in charge, but he wasn't

» **Annas**—the former high priest and Caiaphas's father-in-law

» **Simon of Cyrene**—helped Jesus carry the cross

» **Peter**—a repentant denier

» **Judas**—the ultimate denier and betrayer

WHERE ARE WE?

» **Jerusalem**—where the sacrifices all occurred, from the temple to Jesus himself

» **Mount of Olives**—a mountain of olive trees, like the name says

» **Gethsemane**—where olives were squeezed and prayers squeezed out

» **Golgotha**—where people were crucified; also called "The Skull Place"

 INTERESTING STUFF IN THIS SECTION

» The day Jesus died, Friday, is called Good Friday. While it doesn't seem good, the good that came out of it was—Jesus died for our sins so we could be forgiven.

» For Jews, the Sabbath was Saturday. Sunday was a regular workday.

» The last week of Jesus' earthly life is called the Passion Week. The "Passion" reveals his love and heart for people showed by wanting to sacrifice himself for our sins.

» Passover in Israel would be like Thanksgiving or Christmas in America. It was a huge deal.

» Every time Judas was mentioned in the Bible, so was money. It hints that greed was a big problem for Judas.

Sunday (MATTHEW 21:1–11; MARK 11:1–11; LUKE 19:28–44; JOHN 12:1–19)

It was the day after the Sabbath—Sunday—and everyone had the coming Passover celebration on their mind. Passover was a nationwide holiday that would be starting in just a few days—Thursday—and many people had started coming to Jerusalem.

> Prophecy fulfilled: "Rejoice greatly, Daughter Zion! Shout, Daughter Jerusalem! See, your king comes to you, righteous and victorious, lowly and riding on a donkey, on a colt, the foal of a donkey" (Zechariah 9:9).

Jesus and his followers came to Jerusalem early and stopped in Bethphage and Bethany there on the Mount of Olives. Jesus visited Lazarus, whom he had raised from the dead. Many Jews believed in Jesus because of this miracle.

That day, Jesus sent two disciples into town to find a donkey that had never been ridden and bring it to him. Jesus rode the donkey into Jerusalem. The people shouted, "Hosanna! Blessed is he who comes in the name of the Lord!" They threw

palm branches before him and laid their cloaks on the ground. Everyone thought Jesus had come to conquer the Romans.

No. He had a more important kingdom to fight for.

Monday (MATTHEW 21:12–17; MARK 11:15–19; LUKE 11:15–19; JOHN 12:20–50)

Remember three years ago, when Jesus first started his ministry and walked into the temple and cleared out all the money changers and sellers of lambs and doves for sacrifice? Well, Jesus did it again. Nobody had learned their lesson. Jesus knocked over their tables and sent everyone running. Jesus loved the temple and what it represented, but he hated how the people treated it.

This time the religious leaders were really upset and wanted him dead.

Jesus felt a very important time was coming. He told his followers that when a seed hits the ground, it has to die, crack open, and come to life, a sprout bursting out of it. So too must someone lose their life to save it. Jesus knew he came to earth for this very reason. He looked to heaven and said, "Father, glorify your name!"

> That's three times God spoke from the heavens to those around Jesus.

A voice came from heaven: "I have glorified it and I will again!" The people heard it like thunder.

Jesus turned to the people and said, "I will be lifted up off this earth and draw people to me." He was telling them that he would be lifted up on a cross and his death would draw many to believe in him. Right now, many struggled to believe in him. Some Pharisees started to believe, but they were afraid they would lose their jobs and get kicked out of the temple.

"I didn't come to judge the world," Jesus said, "but to save it. I'm telling you what my Father tells me." That night, Jesus stayed outside Jerusalem because many wanted him dead as soon as possible.

Tuesday (MATTHEW 21:18-25:46; MARK 11:19-13:37; LUKE 20:1-21:36)

Early that morning, as Jesus and his disciples headed toward Jerusalem, they saw a fig tree with no fruit, just leaves. Jesus told the tree it would never produce fruit again. The tree withered.

The disciples wondered how Jesus did that. "If you have faith and don't doubt, you can toss mountains into the sea. You just need to pray."

As they entered the temple courtyard, the chief priests and elders stopped Jesus and asked him where he thought he got all this authority. Jesus asked them a question about authority: "When John baptized, did he get his authority from heaven or earth?" This was a trick question and would make the leaders look bad with either answer.

They told Jesus they didn't know. He responded, "Then I won't tell you where I get my authority."

Jesus went on and told many parables that attacked the Pharisees. The parables about two sons, the tenants who rented out a landowner's property, and the wedding banquet all said that the Pharisees were disobedient and murderers who wouldn't be allowed into heaven. Tax collectors and sinners who believed in and loved Jesus will be there with God for eternity before them.

The religious leaders knew he was talking about them and tried to find a way to arrest him and kill him. However, Jesus was becoming very popular, so they backed off.

Instead, the religious leaders tried to trap Jesus with words. They asked Jesus if they should pay the imperial tax to Caesar, trying to get him into political trouble. He saw through the plan and asked for a coin. He took it and saw the image of Caesar, and said, "Give to Caesar what belongs to Caesar and give to God what belongs to God."

Now it was another group's turn—the Sadducees, who didn't believe in heaven, angels, and life after death. They asked Jesus what happens to a woman whose husband dies and she marries his brother to keep the family inheritance in the family. Then *that* brother dies and she marries another brother, then another, all the way to seven brothers. "So in heaven, whose wife will she be?" The question was ridiculous. Jesus answered, "You don't know Scripture, do you? There's no marriage in heaven."

The Pharisees sent an expert in the law next. "Teacher, what's the greatest commandment in the law?" That one was easy to answer for Jesus. "Love the Lord your God with all your heart and with all your soul and with all your mind. That's first. Second is love your neighbor as much as you love yourself." Everyone agreed that was a good answer.

The Pharisees kept trying to trap Jesus, but it didn't work. Jesus turned the attack around on them, telling them they don't practice what they preach, they just try to make life difficult for everyone else. He told everyone not to call them teachers. Jesus cursed them, calling them hypocrites, blind guides, fools, snakes, and murderers. He said they washed up

> Jesus' increased attacks on the religious leaders sped up their desire to get him to the cross.

and looked nice on the outside, but on the inside they were dirty, wicked, and only out for blood. You can imagine how they felt about Jesus saying that.

Jesus and his disciples walked into the treasury area of the temple, where people dropped off their offerings. Many rich people threw in large amounts for everyone to see. But Jesus spotted a poor widow dropping a couple pennies in the offering and said, "Those others gave out of their wealth. She gave out of her poverty. That was everything she had to live on. She put more in the offering than those rich people."

The group left the temple, where they had a view of the magnificent buildings in Jerusalem and surrounding the temple. Jesus shocked them by saying, "One day this will all be destroyed." The disciples asked when this would happen.

Jesus told them to watch and make sure no one deceived them. He said there will be false prophets, wars, famines, and earthquakes in the future, and they would all be persecuted and put to death. He said there will be betrayal, wickedness, and lies, but the gospel would be preached to the whole world. After that, the end would come. It would be very bad. People running for their lives. It would be unlike anything they've ever seen.

> One day Jesus will return to the earth and take with him those who believe in him.

Jesus emphasized, "Don't listen to any false prophets or people who say they are messiahs! One day I'll be back with a loud, victorious trumpet call! No one knows when that will happen." He said it would be like a thief who surprises the homeowner at night. Jesus told them that even though everything they see will pass away, his words would never pass away.

Jesus then told parables about a faithful and wise servant and a wicked servant whose master was away, ten bridesmaids who were surprised by the arrival of the groom, and three servants who were given bags of gold and told to multiply them. All the stories spoke about not being ready for the arrival of the master, not doing enough to prepare for him. In those stories, anyone who did not serve the master faithfully was tossed out and punished.

Jesus warned them about hell, a place where disobedient, stubborn sinners who refuse to love God, their master, are punished forever, beginning the day death comes for them.

On the day when Jesus returns, it will be like a shepherd who separates the sheep from the goats. The sheep are those who show their love of Jesus by helping others. They will go to be with him forever. The goats are the lovers of self, sin, and Satan, who go to be in hell forever.

"Which do you want? Eternal life or eternal punishment?" Jesus asked them.

Hell is a place where all those who don't believe in Jesus go so they can continue their wish to be apart from him.

That night, with Passover and the Festival of Unleavened Bread only two days away, Jesus reclined at a table in the home of Simon the Leper (apparently someone Jesus healed from leprosy). While there, a woman—Mary, sister of Lazarus—entered with a very expensive jar of perfume. She broke it and let the perfume pour over Jesus' head. It's called an anointing.

Some people around them protested, saying this was a waste of money, worth up to a year's salary. Jesus felt this was a beautiful thing because it prepared him for his burial. Jesus knew he would die very soon, and dead bodies were covered in perfume so they smelled good in the tomb.

Prophecy fulfilled: "I told them, 'If you think it best, give me my pay; but if not, keep it.' So they paid me thirty pieces of silver" (Zechariah 11:12).

Judas Iscariot was in charge of the money for the group, and he didn't like the direction things were going. Judas looked for an opportunity to turn things around. He met with the religious leaders Jesus attacked, and agreed to hand Jesus over for thirty pieces of silver.

The next day, Wednesday, was a quiet day. Thursday, though, would be a very busy and a very important day in history.

Thursday (MATTHEW 26:1-30; MARK 14:1-26; LUKE 22:1-38; JOHN 13-17)

Thursday began the Festival of Unleavened Bread—a day that celebrated the Israelites leaving Egypt, when they made bread but didn't have time to wait for it to rise. God worked quickly to get them to freedom. Jesus would die very quickly: In almost twelve hours, he would be on a cross dying for people's sins and freeing them from death.

Jesus told the disciples to go into Jerusalem to prepare for Passover, which started at sundown. Passover celebrated the Jews in Egypt being protected from death when they put the blood of the lamb on their doorposts so death passed over their homes. They found a room available on the second floor of a house, called an upper room.

Once everyone was seated, Jesus took off his robe and washed the feet of all those in attendance. A servant usually did this, not a rabbi, but Jesus wanted to show them an example of humility.

As Jesus returned to the table, he said that one of them in the group would betray him. They were all shocked, especially Judas. "Certainly not I?" Jesus leaned over and said, "Yes, now go and do what you need to do." Judas left. Judas was their treasurer, so he always left to go pay the bills.

Jesus turned to the others and said, "I am only here a little longer, so I want to tell you to love one another, just as I have loved you."

Peter agreed enthusiastically, but Jesus told him, "Tonight you will betray me three times by the time the rooster crows."

Two items were always on the table for Passover—bread and wine. Jesus took the bread, broke it, and passed it out to the others. He said, "This represents my body. Take it and eat." Then he took the wine and passed the cup, saying, "This represents my blood. Drink and remember me."

> There's only one way to get to God, and that's through a relationship with Jesus. There's no other way!

All this talk about leaving, betrayal, and death bothered his friends around the table. "Don't let your hearts be troubled. I am going to prepare a place for you so one day you can join me." Jesus continued, "I am the way, the truth, and life, and no one can get to the Father except by me."

Jesus described a grapevine with a branch that extends to vines, which produce fruit. He then told them that he was the vine and they were the branches. A follower must be closely attached to him to produce fruit. Jesus promised that the Holy Spirit would come and fill them, teaching them and guiding them while pointing out the world's sins.

Jesus prayed to his Father, glorifying him, then asked God to protect these disciples and the new believers that would come. They sang a song, then went to the Mount of Olives.

Under Arrest (MATTHEW 26:36-56; MARK 14:27-52; LUKE 22:39-51; JOHN 18:1-12)

The Mount of Olives is a mountain on the south side of Jerusalem, close to the temple. Many olive trees grew there, making it a mountain of olive trees. The name of the garden area where Jesus and his disciples met was called Gethsemane, meaning "olive press."

Prophecy fulfilled: "'Awake, sword, against my shepherd, against the man who is close to me!' declares the LORD Almighty. 'Strike the shepherd, and the sheep will be scattered, and I will turn my hand against the little ones'" (Zechariah 13:7).

It's here Jesus felt the pressure of what was about to happen. He asked his apostles to wait nearby and pray, keeping a security watch. Jesus prayed, overcome by grief, "Father, if it's your will, take this from me, but I'm here for your will not mine."

Jesus checked on his disciples. They were all asleep. "Couldn't you stay up for an hour?" Jesus then saw the group coming to arrest him. "Here we go, the Son of Man is about to be turned over to sinners."

Judas burst forth from the crowd and kissed Jesus. It was a signal to the soldiers that this was the guy they wanted.

As the soldiers grabbed Jesus, Peter pulled a sword and swung it, cutting off the ear of a guy named Malchus. Jesus put the man's ear back on, healing him completely.

Then the soldiers tied up Jesus and led him away. The disciples all ran away scared.

Religious Leaders' Trial (MATTHEW 26:57–27:10; MARK 14:53–65; LUKE 22:52–71; JOHN 18:13–28)

Late that night, the soldiers brought Jesus to Annas, the father-in-law of the high priest. He questioned Jesus about his teaching. Jesus told him he had nothing to hide.

One of the officials slapped Jesus, finding his answer disrespectful.

"If I spoke the truth, why did you hit me?" Jesus asked his attacker.

Annas sent him chained up to Caiaphas, the acting high priest. Many teachers and members of the Sanhedrin were there. They

> Prophecy fulfilled: "He was oppressed and afflicted, yet he did not open his mouth; he was led like a lamb to the slaughter, and as a sheep before its shearers is silent, so he did not open his mouth" (Isaiah 53:7).

wanted to find something wrong with Jesus but could not. They talked to a few witnesses who told lies about

Jesus, saying he wanted to tear down the temple and build a new kingdom.

They asked Jesus to defend himself. He kept silent.

Caiaphas pressured Jesus. "If you are the Messiah, the son of God, tell us!"

Jesus calmly answered, "I am, but you won't believe me. And one day you'll see me sitting on the throne next to God."

Everybody went crazy, saying he spoke against God, thinking he was equal to God! "He must die!" They spit in his face, blindfolded him, punched and slapped him.

Meanwhile, Peter stood outside in the courtyard, watching everything from a distance. It was cold so many gathered around a fire. A servant girl looked at him and recognized he was with Jesus of Nazareth. Peter denied it, saying, "I don't know what you're talking about."

Peter stepped away, but another servant girl recognized him as a friend of Jesus. Peter again denied. "I don't know the man!"

Then a group walked up and one of them accused Peter of cutting off his relative's ear. Peter screamed, cursing, swearing that he did not know this man!

Right then, a rooster crowed. Peter remembered what Jesus had said—that Peter would deny Jesus three times before the rooster crowed. Peter ran away crying.

While this happened, Judas started to feel very guilty about what he did, betraying Jesus and handing him over to the religious leaders. Judas went to the people who paid him, and he threw the bags of silver at them. Judas ran away and hanged himself. Nobody wanted to touch the body of a cursed man.

Roman Interrogation (MATTHEW 27:11-30; MARK 15:1-20; LUKE 23:1-25; JOHN 18:29-19:16)

The Jewish religious leaders could have stoned Jesus, but they wanted him crucified like a common criminal, so they decided to take him to Pilate, the Roman governor and most powerful person in the area. They pushed Jesus before him and said that he refused to pay taxes and claimed to be a king. According to the Romans, Caesar was the only king.

Pilate asked Jesus, "Are you king of the Jews?"

"I am," Jesus replied. Pilate didn't see anything wrong with a person thinking that.

The leaders pushed on. "He stirs people up all over Judea and Galilee."

Pilate heard the word *Galilee* and sent Jesus to Herod Antipas, the son of Herod the Great, who ruled over the Jews but really had no power. Herod happened to be in Jerusalem at the time.

Herod had wanted to meet Jesus for a long time. He hoped Jesus would perform a sign or something cool, but Jesus did nothing and refused to answer any questions. Herod got mad and had his soldiers mock and beat Jesus, put a robe on him, and dress him up like a king.

Herod sent Jesus back to Pilate. Pilate said again he couldn't find any basis to crucify Jesus. But the Jewish religious leaders yelled and screamed.

Pilate remembered a custom he used to do where he released one prisoner on Passover. It was something that made the people happy. Pilate offered to release either Jesus or Barabbas, a man arrested for rebellion and murder. The people shouted, "We want Barabbas!" Pilate released a murderer instead of an innocent man.

Pilate's wife came to Pilate and said she had a bad dream the night before. She warned Pilate not to have anything to do with this innocent man.

Pilate wanted Jesus released but the people insisted. "Crucify him! Crucify him!" they cried. Pilate wondered why; Jesus had done nothing wrong.

He turned to Jesus and asked, "Are you king of the Jews?"

Jesus replied, "Is that your own idea or did someone else tell you that? My kingdom is not of this world. Those who know the truth know who I am."

Pilate shook his head. "What is truth?"

Pilate decided to torture Jesus, so he turned Jesus over to the soldiers, who whipped him and showed no mercy. The guards created a crown made of thorns, since every "king" needs a crown, then pushed it onto his head. They slapped him and made fun of him, mockingly bowing to him like to a king.

Then Pilate showed Jesus to everyone. "Here is the man who thinks he's your king." Pilate hoped torturing Jesus would be enough to satisfy the crowd and he could let Jesus go. But the Pharisees had been stirring up the crowd ahead of time, so now everyone turned on Pilate—even the ones who had been cheering him on not long ago. "Crucify him! Crucify him! Our king is Caesar!"

With nothing else to do and afraid the crowd would riot, Pilate turned Jesus over to be crucified.

The Crucifixion (MATTHEW 27:31-56; MARK 15:20-40; LUKE 23:26-49; JOHN 19:17-37)

First Three Hours

Jesus was severely beaten by the Roman soldiers, then stripped of his clothes to almost nothing and told to carry his cross through the streets. A cross was a big wooden T that they hung people on to die. The weight of the big beam of wood was too much for Jesus after his beatings, so the guards pulled a guy named Simon from the town of Cyrene to help him.

When they arrived at Golgotha (which means "place of the skull"), they drove nails into Jesus' hands and feet,

Prophecy fulfilled: "But he was pierced for our transgressions, he was crushed for our iniquities; the punishment that brought us peace was on him, and by his wounds we are healed" (Isaiah 53:5).

securing him to the cross and lifting him to bleed to death and die in the sun.

As was the custom, they put a sign over his head to tell everyone his crime. "This is Jesus: The king of the Jews." It was about nine in the morning.

On both sides of Jesus were two criminals who mocked Jesus, as did many other who walked by. The chief priests and teachers of the law hurled insults at him: "He saved others but he can't save himself!" and, "If you're so special, come down off the cross and show us!"

Over time, one of the criminals next to Jesus began to understand who Jesus was. He defended Jesus against the accusers, then said to Jesus, "Don't forget me when you enter your kingdom." Jesus promised, "Today, you'll be with me in paradise."

As he hung there dying, Jesus told the apostle John to take care of his mother.

He looked down on his accusers and torturers and said, "Father, forgive them, because they don't really know what they're doing."

Final Three Hours

From noon to three, everything started to get dark. Jesus cried out, "My God, my God, why have you forsaken me?" Jesus felt alone. He was thirsty.

Jesus cried out, "Father, into your hands I give my spirit!"

Then, taking his final breaths, Jesus said, "It is finished."

At that moment, an earthquake shook the land.

The veil in the temple that separated God from the people tore open.

Graves opened up, and dead people who loved God came to life.

A Roman centurion who had seen many crucifixions knew this one was different. "Surely he was the Son of God," he muttered.

But to make sure Jesus was dead, they drove a spear into his chest.

> Prophecy fulfilled: "Yet it was the LORD's will to crush him and cause him to suffer, and though the LORD makes his life an offering for sin, he will see his offspring and prolong his days, and the will of the LORD will prosper in his hand" (Isaiah 53:10).

Many followers of Jesus, mostly women, watched this all from a distance—including Mary, his mother; Mary

Magdalene; and others. A few of them would help put Jesus in the grave . . . a grave he refused to stay in.

WHAT'S THE POINT?

► Jesus died on the Passover to show that his death, like the sacrificial lamb, guaranteed that the believer would not die, but death would "pass over" those who put their faith in Jesus.

► Jesus suffered death to the extreme. He was betrayed, abandoned, mocked, spat on, punched, stabbed, unfairly convicted, you name it. Jesus can identify with the way in which many people die on this earth.

► Jesus was very forgiving and kind to others as he died, even to those who put him on the cross.

► The earth shook and the sky went dark upon the death of Jesus, who had come to the earth to show love and sacrifice. Jesus' death really shook things up!

► Most of those who stayed with Jesus until the end were women.

18

He's Back

MATTHEW 28; MARK 16; LUKE 24; JOHN 20-21

WHO'S WHO

» **Jesus**—you can't keep a good man down

» **Joseph of Arimathea**—a rich man who lends his tomb to Jesus for three days

» **Nicodemus**—the Pharisee returned to help bury Jesus

» **Mary Magdalene**—she gets the award for being the first to see Jesus resurrected

» **Thomas**—the doubter who got all the proof he needed

» **Peter**—the coward becomes the leader

WHERE ARE WE?

» **Jerusalem**—where dead people walk

» **Upper Room**—the disciples' hiding place

» **Road to Emmaus**—where Jesus went on a stroll

» **Galilee**—Jesus stopped in to do some fishing

INTERESTING STUFF IN THIS SECTION

» A resurrection is a body coming back to life in a new, eternal form. Lazarus' old body was resurrected, but that old body eventually died. Jesus' resurrected body is ready for eternity and will never die. It's the body all believers will one day receive.

» Jesus is the only person in history with a resurrected body.

» Paul, a writer in the New Testament, said that over five hundred people saw Jesus in resurrected form during those forty days. That's pretty good proof.

» Jews counted a day as any part of that day, not a total of twenty-four hours. Jesus died on Friday (one day), was in the tomb all day Saturday, then rose again on Sunday morning (one day). That's three days, although not seventy-two total hours.

Friday Afternoon (MATTHEW 27:55-66; MARK 15:40-47; LUKE 23:49-56; JOHN 19:21-42)

The big celebration of Passover began at sundown, and Jews needed to be in their homes by that time. Friday was a preparation day, to prepare for the Sabbath. There was a mad scramble to get things done before 5 p.m. so they didn't need to work on the Sabbath.

Joseph of Arimathea, a rich man and member of the Sanhedrin, asked for the body of Jesus. He secretly had become a follower of Jesus. Pilate gave him permission, and he took the body away, helped by Nicodemus, the Pharisee who met Jesus that one night.

They covered Jesus' body in fragrances and perfumes, such as frankincense and myrrh, then wrapped Jesus with cloths to pack it all in. These spices weighed almost seventy-five pounds, the amount that would be used to bury a king!

Joseph was rich and had a tomb recently carved in the stone for his family. A tomb was like a small room that someone could walk into and place numerous bodies. Jesus was the first body put into that tomb.

> Interesting that two of the gifts the wise men gave were used in the burial of Jesus.

A few followers of Jesus, all women, watched Joseph and Nicodemus, and saw where Jesus was laid. They rolled a stone in front of the tomb to keep people out and ran home before sundown.

A few of the Jewish leaders remembered Jesus talking about rising from the dead. They didn't want the apostles to secretly remove Jesus' body and tell stories that he had risen, so they asked Pilate for guards to be put around the tomb. Pilate agreed, and Rome's finest parked themselves outside to keep people out.

> **Prophecy fulfilled:**
>
> "He was assigned a grave with the wicked, and with the rich in his death, though he had done no violence, nor was any deceit in his mouth" (Isaiah 53:9).

But they couldn't keep someone in. . . .

Saturday

There's nothing written about what happened on Saturday, but since it was a Sabbath, it would be a day of no work and reflection on what Passover was all about. The apostles stayed in the Upper Room they rented on Thursday. Jews did not go anywhere because Saturday was a Sabbath.

Sunday Morning (MATTHEW 28:1-8; MARK 16:1-8; LUKE 24:1-12; JOHN 20:1-10)

As soon as the sun rose, Jews could leave their homes and walk around. This was the first possible moment anyone could visit the tomb. A few women decided to visit to replenish the fragrances and spices around the body—a custom the family did so their loved one's decomposing body would not smell.

> Resurrected Jesus first appeared to women, showing how important women are to God.

The first witnesses—Mary Magdalene, Joanna, Mary the mother of James and Joseph, Salome the mother of James and John, and several other women—arrived at the tomb during sunrise to cover Jesus' body with perfumes. As they walked to the tomb, they wondered who could help them remove the stone, which could weigh three hundred pounds.

When they arrived, the stone was already rolled away. How did this happen? Just moments before, a great

earthquake had struck the area as an angel descended from heaven and moved the stone. The Roman guards, some of the toughest guys around, became scared, shaking, their faces turning white. They ran away.

The women were not afraid and looked into the tomb. No Jesus. Only a young man dressed in a white robe was sitting inside. He told them, "You are looking for Jesus. He's not here. He has risen. See where they laid his body. Now go and tell his disciples, and especially Peter."

They ran, shaking with excitement.

The women entered the Upper Room and began talking over each other, trying to tell the news. What they said made no sense to the men. "Jesus . . . alive . . . empty . . . angel . . . tomb . . . risen!" What did all this mean?

Peter and John bolted out first, running as fast as they could to the tomb. Inside, they found the strips of linen used to wrap Jesus, nicely folded. They instantly believed. Jesus was alive! They ran back to tell the others.

Jesus' Appearances (MATTHEW 28:9-20; MARK 16:9-20; LUKE 24:13-53; JOHN 20:11-21:25)

In total, Jesus appeared to over five hundred people over his forty days in resurrected form. Here are stories about some of the people he met.

The Other Mary Did Know

As Peter and John ran back, Mary Magdalene found herself outside the tomb, crying. She looked inside for herself and saw two angels. They asked why she was crying. Mary was sad that Jesus was taken away.

> Jesus' resurrected body looked like Jesus, but he was not recognizable at first.

Suddenly, a voice came from behind her. "Why are you crying? Who are you looking for?" She thought the person was the gardener. After Mary explained, the person said, "Mary."

She knew the sound of that voice. Jesus! She yelled, "Teacher!" and fell at his feet, holding on. Jesus told her she couldn't hold on because he was returning to his Father and God, who was now her Father and God.

Mary Magdalene ran to the Upper Room to tell the others that she had seen the Lord.

The Cover-Up

The guards reported to the chief priests what had happened (the earthquake, angel, and rock), but they didn't want that story to get out. So they bribed the guards to keep it quiet and tell everyone the disciples came and stole the body. That story became very popular around town, even to today.

Two Disciples on the Road to Emmaus

Two of Jesus' disciples were walking to a village named Emmaus, about seven miles outside of Jerusalem. They discussed all the things that had happened recently with Jesus—his death and even his disappearance from the grave, which some women had claimed happened.

Then a stranger walked alongside them and asked what they were talking about. They filled him in on everything, adding that their friends went to the tomb and verified that Jesus was missing.

The stranger explained many things from what we now know as the Bible, and they were very interested in what he had to say, so they invited him to dinner. At dinner, the stranger took the bread, broke it, and gave thanks, just like Jesus did. Their eyes were opened; they realized this was no stranger—it was their friend Jesus. Suddenly, he disappeared. They ran back to Jerusalem and found the apostles in the Upper Room and told them the news.

> Jesus' resurrected body could disappear and reappear, from place to place and through locked doors.

"It's true! The Lord has risen!"

The Upper Room Crew

One night, while all the disciples hid inside the room for fear of the Jewish leaders, Jesus appeared in front of them. "Peace be with you," he said, showing them the nail holes in his hands and feet to prove it was really him.

Jesus breathed on them, sending the Holy Spirit into them, and sending them out to go and tell others.

Thomas Time

Unfortunately, during Jesus' first visit to the Upper Room, Thomas wasn't there. When Thomas returned, the disciples told him that Jesus was alive. Thomas replied, "I won't believe until I see the nail marks with my own eyes."

A week later, the disciples were all in the room again, this time with Thomas. The doors were locked like last time, but Jesus appeared in the room again.

He turned to Thomas and said, "Put your finger in these nail holes. Look at where they stabbed me. It's me. You can stop doubting and start believing."

Thomas fell to his knees, convinced. "My Lord and my God!" he cried.

Jesus said, "You've seen me and now believed. How blessed will be those people who don't see me and yet believe."

Big Fish Catch, Part 2

Peter, Thomas, Nathanael, James, John, and two others were fishing in the Sea of Galilee. They went out while it was dark but caught nothing.

As they rowed toward the shore in the morning, someone on the coastline asked if they caught anything. They said no.

The stranger said, "Throw your net on the right side of the boat and you'll catch some." They did, and the nets filled to capacity with fish.

John shouted, remembering the miracle that first got their attention. "It's the Lord!" Peter jumped in the water and swam to Jesus to welcome him.

Jesus had a fire going and some fish and bread cooking, another reminder of a miracle. They gathered around and ate. This made three times Jesus had visited them since the resurrection.

As they finished eating, Jesus turned to Peter and said, "Do you love me?"

Peter said, "Yes, you know that."

Jesus replied, "Good, feed my lambs."

A little later, Jesus asked the same question. Peter affirmed his love.

Jesus then said, "Take care of my sheep."

A third time, Jesus asked if Peter loved him. By now, Peter was stressing out. "Yes, yes, you know I do."

Jesus replied a third time, "Feed my sheep."

Jesus was forgiving Peter for the three denials, through three expressions of love. Jesus trusted Peter to take care of his flock, his people, who needed guidance once Jesus departed.

One Last Time in Galilee

Jesus met the eleven disciples up on a mountain in Galilee. They worshiped him. Jesus gave them instructions to carry out once he left this earth.

He said, "All authority has been given to me, so go and make disciples of all nations, baptizing them in the name of the Father and of the Son and of the Holy Spirit. Teach them to obey everything I've said. Don't worry. I'll be with you. Always."

Next Stop, Heaven

Later, near Bethany on the Mount of Olives, Jesus took his disciples up the mountain. He lifted his hands and blessed them.

Then Jesus was taken up into the sky to sit at the right hand of God his Father. The disciples worshiped and sang, praising God for all they saw.

The next time Jesus comes to earth will be the end of the earth and the beginning of a new earth and new heaven! Come soon, Jesus!

It's hard to believe, but Jesus did many more things, but there just wasn't room in all the books ever printed to describe every one of them.

WHAT'S THE POINT?

▶ The resurrection is what our faith is all about. It's the most important event in history. Why? Because it proved that Jesus was who he said he was—God, the Messiah, our Savior. Nobody has ever accurately predicted their own rising from the dead.

▶ The Bible says that without the resurrection, our faith is empty and useless. Without the resurrection, there's no reason to go to church, or read the Bible or this book.

▶ Many people try to explain away the resurrection through stories, just like the story the guards came up with about the disciples stealing Jesus' body. That's even believed today! Remember, if Satan can cause us to doubt the resurrection, he wins.

► What Jesus told the disciples to do before he left is the same instructions that we should do also: tell people the good news, help them accept Jesus as their Lord and Savior, and teach them to be followers of God.

19

Let's Go to Church

ACTS

 WHO'S WHO

» **Jesus**—still in charge, still changing lives

» **Peter**—delivered the first sermon that started the first church

» **Stephen**—the first person to die for Jesus

» **Philip**—the first person to fly from one place to another without a plane

» **Ethiopian official**—was reading his Bible while driving his chariot

» **Paul**, who was formerly known as Saul the church destroyer, becomes the church builder

» **Cornelius**—visited by an angel and Peter and became the first Gentile believer

» **Barnabas**—a nice, encouraging guy

WHERE ARE WE?

» **Jerusalem**—everyone runs from here to start churches all over the world

» **Antioch**—people were first called Christians here

» **Various places and islands**—Acts takes us to so many places it's like a show on the Travel Channel

 ## INTERESTING STUFF IN THIS SECTION

» The book of Acts shows the actions of the apostles to bring the truth about Jesus to many people and create churches throughout the land.

» A church is defined as a gathering of people united by their belief in Jesus, not a building where people attend. There were no church buildings in those days, only homes and open courtyards where people would meet to pray and preach.

» Christianity was originally called the Way, because of Jesus' statement in John 14:6.

» Luke wrote Acts. He gathered information and wrote Acts chapters 1-15, but in chapter 16 Luke uses words like "we" and "us," meaning he joined Paul on his missionary journey.

» Three continents are covered in Acts: Asia, Europe, and Africa.

» Saul was Paul's Jewish name. Paul was his Roman/non-Jewish name. Since Paul worked to reach non-Jews, his preferred name was Paul.

See You Later Jesus, Hello Holy Spirit (ACTS 1–3)

Forty days after Jesus' resurrection, after walking away and showing himself to the disciples, Jesus gave his followers a command: Don't leave Jerusalem until you receive a gift from God . . . the Holy Spirit.

He stood on the Mount of Olives, the same place where he was arrested, and said to the disciples, "You will receive power from the Holy Spirit, and then you will be witnesses about what you've seen in Jerusalem, Judea, Samaria, and all over the earth."

Then Jesus was taken up into the sky.

The disciples stood there and watched the clouds, amazed by what they saw. Two angels appeared and said, "Why are you guys standing around and looking at the sky? He'll be back one day."

The apostles went to the Upper Room and began to pray. Even Jesus' mom, Mary, joined them. They decided to replace the betrayer Judas with a new apostle. They voted on a man named Matthias.

Fifty days later, Pentecost was first celebrated when the Jews started the harvest. A number of believers were together, and a sound like wind blowing filled the house, and little flames of fire appeared over their heads. As the Holy Spirit filled them, they began talking in languages they did not understand. People standing around recognized their language because they were from those places.

Peter stood before a huge crowd and told the people that the Old Testament knew this day would happen. He

quoted Scripture that said God would pour out his Spirit on the people one day, and today was that day!

He explained the story of Jesus: God himself coming to earth and being handed over to wicked men who killed him on the cross. But it was impossible for death to stop him. While other great leaders like David died, only one stepped out of the grave, resurrected, and is now sitting at God's right hand.

The people understood and asked what they should do. Peter said, "Repent of your sins so you can be forgiven, then be baptized. The Holy Spirit will fill you." The Holy Spirit is one of the three persons of God, and he lives in people who trust in Jesus.

Prophecy fulfilled:

"And afterward, I will pour out my Spirit on all people.
Your sons and daughters will prophesy, your old men will dream dreams, your young men will see visions" (Joel 2:28).

Let's Go to Church

Three thousand people agreed, repented, and were baptized that day. Immediately they began to meet together, enjoying the messages from the apostles, eating with one another, praying. Many signs and wonders happened. The people shared everything they had with one another, and nobody had a need. Day after day, more people got saved.

Peter Lights a Fire (ACTS 4-6)

One day, Peter and John were going to the temple when they saw a man who had not walked since birth. He asked them for money. Peter did not give him money, but rather, in the name of Jesus, the ability to walk. The man jumped to his feet and began to praise God.

Everyone who saw this and knew the man was surprised. Peter asked, "Why are you surprised? It's in Jesus' name and by faith he has been healed." Peter told them to repent of their sins and put their faith in the Messiah who Moses and the prophets promised would one day come to the earth. Many believed, growing the total number of followers to five thousand.

The priests and temple guards arrested Peter and John and took them to the Sanhedrin, the Jewish "Supreme Court." Annas, the high priest who met with Jesus, asked Peter and John, "By whose name are you doing all this?"

"The name of Jesus," Peter replied. "The man you crucified and God raised from the dead. Only by his name can you be saved."

These religious leaders saw how courageous and wise these unschooled, ordinary men were. They knew if Peter and John did more miracles, everyone would believe in their truth and stop following the religious leaders. So they told Peter and John to stop talking about Jesus.

Peter and John replied, "There's no way. We cannot stop speaking about everything we saw!" After more threats, the Sanhedrin let them go.

The church praised God as they heard Peter and John's story. As they prayed, the room shook and people were filled with the Holy Spirit. The people shared their possessions so nobody was needy, including a man named Barnabas, who sold a field he owned so he could give the money to the apostles.

While the Holy Spirit told people to share, Satan was telling others to cheat. A married couple named Ananias and Sapphira also sold some land they owned, but they kept some of the money for themselves. When they lied about the money, God struck them dead. God did not want any sin to creep into the church.

While Peter and the apostles healed many

people in Jerusalem, the high priests became jealous and had them all arrested. But during the night, an angel opened the jail doors and walked them out. The angel told them to go to the temple and tell people about Jesus.

The high priest and all the Sanhedrin asked for the apostles to be brought to them, but nobody could find them in jail. Somebody said, "Look, they're in the temple courts teaching everyone!" Again, the apostles were arrested and brought before the high priest.

The apostles refused to listen to these men. "We can only obey God, not you. This message of forgiveness of sins is too important." At first the Jewish leaders wanted to kill them, but after talking amongst themselves, they decided to have them whipped, then sent away, telling them not to speak about Jesus.

The apostles rejoiced that they could suffer like Jesus, then went back to the temple courts, teaching and speaking the good news that Jesus had come to save them!

Stephen Sees Jesus in Heaven (ACTS 6-7)

As the number of followers of Jesus increased, including priests, more and more work fell on the apostles. Not only were they preaching, but also handing out food to widows every day. They decided to choose deacons—those full of the Spirit and wisdom—to hand out the food. Seven deacons were chosen, including Stephen and Philip.

Stephen especially performed great wonders and signs. He showed God's grace and power, and when his critics began to argue with him, they could not win because of his wisdom. So they found some men to bring false accusations against him. When they brought Stephen before the Sanhedrin, his face was like an angel.

He told the Jewish leaders about the history of the Bible, from Abraham to Joseph and Moses to David. Stephen said people have always opposed God, and these Pharisees were no different. They have always been stubborn, heartless, and deaf, murdering good people all the time.

This made them really mad and made them grind their teeth. As they picked up rocks, Stephen looked to the sky and saw Jesus at the right hand of God. His enemies covered their ears, rushed him, and dragged him out of the city, tossing stones at him and killing him.

A man named Saul stood by, approving what he saw. This man Saul, also known as Paul, began breaking up churches and dragging its leaders off to prison. He became a big problem, so many believers ran out of Jerusalem to other parts of Israel, Asia, and around the world.

Philip Takes Off (ACTS 8)

Philip, another of the deacons, went to Samaria and preached about Jesus there. He performed signs, cast out demons, and healed sickness, and people were overjoyed. A sorcerer named Simon followed Philip, and even he believed and was baptized.

Peter and John visited Samaria after hearing the wonderful news that other people were receiving Jesus. They laid their hands on people to help them receive the Holy Spirit. Simon the Sorcerer wanted to pay Peter and John for their power. Peter scolded him, saying money can't buy God's power, so repent!

An angel sent Philip down the road to meet an Ethiopian official in charge of the queen's treasury. He was in a chariot, reading the book of Isaiah. Philip asked if he understood what it said.

"How can I," the Ethiopian said, "unless someone explains it?"

Philip happily explained Isaiah and the prophecies that pointed to

> Many believe this Ethiopian helped to bring the gospel to Africa.

a Messiah who came to fulfill those prophecies and save all people. The Ethiopian believed and Philip baptized him. Then the Spirit took Philip away and put him in a city called Azotus, where he continued to preach the good news.

Saul Sees the Light (ACTS 9)

Saul went from church to church, threatening to murder anyone who believed in Jesus. He headed to Damascus to find more believers and put them in prison.

Along the way, a bright light flashed from heaven, and Jesus' voice said, "Saul, why are you persecuting me?" Saul recognized Jesus as Lord, and Jesus said, "Now get up and go to Damascus."

Saul found himself blind. For three days he sat in Damascus unable to see. God called a man named Ananias to find Saul and pray for him. He was scared of Saul but did it anyway, and healed Saul's blindness. Saul got baptized and spent a few days with other disciples.

Saul even started preaching, telling his story. People were amazed, remembering him as this church buster, now a church planter. His enemies wanted him dead, but the believers hid him and helped him escape to Jerusalem. Barnabas took him to the apostles, who cautiously watched him.

But Saul amazed everyone, preaching fearlessly, debating, and once again escaping death. With Saul now on the side of the church, the church was at peace and began to grow.

Peter's Animal Dream (ACTS 10-12)

Peter traveled around the country to places such as Lydda and Joppa. He healed a paralyzed man named Aeneas. He raised a dead woman named Tabitha (also known as Dorcas). People believed in God because of these miracles.

While Peter stayed at the house of a guy named Simon, Cornelius, a Roman centurion and believer in God, was in Caesarea and heard an angel tell him to go to Joppa and find Peter. At the same time, Peter had a vision of a sheet lowering from the sky, full of animals, many of them unclean for the Jewish diet. Then he heard a voice that said, "Get up, kill, and eat." Peter protested, but God said, "Do not call anything unclean that God has called clean."

Right then, Cornelius's people showed up to take Peter to see the centurion. Peter told the vision to Cornelius and now understood what the vision meant. Peter needed to take the gospel to the non-Jews (aka Gentiles) like Cornelius. He had to stop playing favorites with the Jews.

Peter went on to tell everyone that he and other apostles witnessed this Jesus and his good deeds of healing and power. They saw him killed on a cross, then God raised him from the dead on the third day. This Jesus is our judge and the Promised One, spoken about by the prophets. As Peter spoke, the Holy Spirit entered the hearts of everyone who heard. They spoke and praised God!

The persecution of Stephen pushed the church to many nations. In Jerusalem, the church sent Barnabas to Antioch. He was a good person, full of faith. Barnabas went to Tarsus to find Saul and bring him to Antioch. It's the first place where believers were called Christians.

King Herod arrested church leaders, putting James (John's brother) to death by a sword. Seeing how the Jews liked this, Herod had Peter arrested. The church started praying for Peter. The night before his trial, Peter, surrounded by guards and bound with chains, was awakened by an angel and told to follow him. The chains fell off and Peter walked out of prison. No one woke up as the locked doors opened.

Peter went to the house where they were praying, but nobody believed it was him. He kept knocking, and when they recognized him, they welcomed him in.

Herod had all the guards killed for being so sloppy. Later, he addressed the people and they shouted, "This is the voice of a God, not a man!" Since Herod did not give praise to God, he died. The word of God spread to the hearts of more and more people.

Paul's First Mission Trip (ACTS 13-14)

The Holy Spirit told leaders in the church of Antioch to send Paul and Barnabas to reach people for Jesus. The leaders prayed over them and sent them off, joined by a guy named John Mark.

They visited Seleucia, Cyprus, Salamis, then Paphos. There they met a Jewish sorcerer and false prophet named Elymas, who worked for Sergius Paulus. Elymas tried to stop them from talking to Sergius Paulus, so Paul called him a child of the devil, and the sorcerer became blind.

Sergius Paulus saw this and believed in God.

Paul and Barnabas traveled to Perga, where John Mark suddenly left them. Then they went to Pisidian Antioch, where they spoke in a synagogue. Paul gave a detailed history of the Jews, John the Baptist, and the message of forgiveness offered through the death and resurrection of Jesus. Many Jews followed Paul and Barnabas, wanting to hear more. Other Jews were jealous of the attention they received and argued with them.

The word of the Lord spread throughout the land. The Jewish leaders stirred up trouble and persecuted Paul and Barnabas. But Paul and Barnabas picked themselves up and left, filled with joy and the Holy Spirit.

In the city of Iconium, Paul and Barnabas went to the local synagogue, but their enemies created false rumors and division, plotting to kill them. They escaped to the cities of Lystra and Derbe.

In Lystra, Paul healed a man who could not walk, and the people thought their gods of Zeus and Hermes had arrived. Paul cried out, "We're just people like you. Let me tell you about the real God!" Rebel Jews

> The first person recorded in the Bible that Paul led to Jesus was named Sergius Paulus, a Gentile and Roman governor.
> Elymas was blinded as Paul had been blinded on the Damascus Road.

> Paul healed a man who could not walk just as Peter had healed a man who could not walk.

from other cities talked the crowd into hating Paul and Barnabas, so they threw rocks at Paul. Thinking that he was dead, they dragged him out of the city. But when the disciples had gathered around him, Paul got up and went back into the city.

The next day, Paul and Barnabas went back to Derbe. Many heard the gospel and gave their lives to Jesus. They visited the cities they had already been to, to check on the believers. They arrived back in Antioch, where they started, and told everyone of the amazing journey, especially how God had opened the door of faith to the Gentiles. The church rejoiced.

Big Conference in Jerusalem (ACTS 15)

Many people during that time believed that a person had to become a Jew in order to become a Christian. They asked Paul and Barnabas to settle the argument. A number of apostles and church leaders gathered to discuss the issue in Jerusalem. They were all very happy that non-Jews (Gentiles) were giving their lives to Christ.

They talked about God's grace allowing people to get saved, and it wasn't by adding any extra work or effort. Why did everyone want to make salvation so difficult?

In the end, they agreed that these Gentiles needed to stay away from certain things after they were saved to show that God had changed their hearts. They wrote a letter to all the churches.

Paul and Barnabas went to Antioch to deliver the letter. The people read it and loved its encouraging message. In

Antioch, Paul and Barnabas decided to take a second missionary journey. They got into a heated argument over John Mark, the man who left them suddenly on their first journey. Paul did not trust him. Barnabas wanted to give him a second chance. So they split up—Barnabas and John Mark

> This seems sad that the friends split up over an argument, but we know from Paul's letters that they were still friends. In fact, this disagreement created two teams that went out to spread the gospel.

(also referred to as Mark) sailed to Cyprus while Paul and a man named Silas started a second missionary journey.

Paul's Second Mission Trip (ACTS 16–18:22)

Paul and Silas went to Derbe, then to Lystra, where a disciple named Timothy lived. Many people liked him and so did Paul, so Timothy joined them. They encouraged churches and delivered the decision made in Jerusalem.

Paul received a vision of a man telling him to come to Macedonia (today Greece). They traveled through regions such as Phrygia, Galatia, Troas, Samothrace, Neapolis, and

> Paul would later write two letters to Timothy, whom he sent to Corinth and Thessalonica. Later, Timothy would be the pastor of the church in Ephesus.

Philippi, a big city in Macedonia. They met with women in a place of prayer and led a businesswoman named Lydia to Jesus.

A fortune-telling slave woman started following Paul around and bothering him. Paul commanded the evil spirit to come out of her and it did. Her owners could no longer make money off her fortune-telling, so they stirred a mob against Paul and his missionaries. The local authorities had Paul and his companions whipped and beaten, then thrown into jail.

At midnight, while Paul and Silas prayed and sang hymns in jail, a violent earthquake broke open the prison doors. The jailer woke up and feared he would be killed, thinking the prisoners had escaped. "We're all here," Paul shouted. The jailer thanked them and then asked how to get saved. "Believe in Jesus," Paul told him. He did and took Paul to his house so his family could get saved, too.

Paul made the local officials apologize for beating and throwing them in prison without a trial. The officials apologized and allowed Paul and Silas to leave prison. They went to Lydia's house to rest and encourage the new believers.

Their travels took them through Amphipolis, Apollonia, then Thessalonica, another city in Greece. As usual, Paul went to the local Jewish synagogue and spoke from the Scriptures about the Messiah. He showed them how Jesus fulfilled all the Old Testament promises. Many Jews and Greeks, especially women, believed.

Other Jews were jealous that so many left their faith, so they formed a mob to search for Paul and Silas, who by now had escaped to another town in Greece called Berea.

The Bereans were smarter people and really listened to what Paul said. They studied and examined the Scriptures. A great many believed. Then those angry Jews in Thessalonica heard where Paul and Silas were, and they sent another angry mob to attack them. Paul went to Athens, while Silas and Timothy stayed in Berea.

The streets of Athens were full of places to worship idols. Paul spoke and debated with Jews and Greeks. A group of philosophers were curious about his message and took him to the Areopagus for a conference. Paul said he could tell these were very religious people, worshiping many things, including an unknown god. He then told them about the God he knew, Jesus, whom God had raised from the dead. When Paul told them about the resurrection, some thought he was crazy and sneered at him. But others became followers of Paul and believed.

Paul left Athens and went to Corinth, in southern Greece. He met a man named Aquila and his wife, Priscilla. Like Paul, they made tents for a living and they worked together. Weekly, Paul spoke in the synagogue, trying to persuade Jews and Greeks to believe in Jesus. Many became believers, including Crispus, the synagogue leader, and his entire family.

> Paul got a haircut at Cenchrea, apparently fulfilling a Nazirite vow taken at Corinth.

Silas and Timothy met Paul in Corinth. But the crowds became abusive. Paul wanted to leave, but in a vision, he heard the Lord tell him to stay and preach. Paul ended up staying a year and a half, despite opposition.

Paul sailed to Syria with Priscilla and Aquila. They stopped in Ephesus, where Priscilla and Aquila stayed. Paul sailed on to Caesarea and finally to Jerusalem and back to Antioch, where his second mission trip ended.

Paul's Third Mission Trip (ACTS 18:23-20:38)

Paul spent time in Antioch, then set out on his third mission trip, to Galatia and Phrygia.

In Ephesus, a man named Apollos arrived. He knew the Scriptures, even taught accurately about Jesus, but he did not know about the Holy Spirit. Priscilla and Aquila taught him things he didn't know. Apollos became a very good debater for Jesus.

Paul arrived in Ephesus and also taught about the baptism of the Holy Spirit. Many believed and received the Holy Spirit. He spoke and argued about the kingdom of God in the local synagogue and a lecture hall for two years. Many extraordinary miracles occurred through Paul, including healings and evil spirits leaving people.

Some Jews tried to cast out demons like Paul did, but they failed miserably. The demons embarrassed them. Many became afraid, including sorcerers who burned their expensive scrolls that showed them how to practice sorcery. People in Ephesus worshiped the goddess Artemis, and they made money by making little idols and trinkets, but they had started losing money because so many believed in Jesus. A silversmith named Demetrius started a riot in Ephesus; the people shouted, "Great is Artemis!" Paul wanted to speak to the crowd, but his friends didn't think it was safe. The city clerk told the crowd to do this peacefully and bring charges against Paul and his companions. Since Paul really did nothing wrong, the crowd went away.

Eutychus's name means "lucky," and he was lucky that Paul was the guest speaker that Sunday.

Paul left Ephesus and traveled to Macedonia, Greece, and Troas with many of his most trusted followers. In Troas, Paul spoke late into the night. One man named Eutychus sat on a windowsill listening, but he fell asleep and fell out the window to his death.

Paul threw himself on Eutychus and brought him back to life.

Paul wanted to go back to Jerusalem, then make his way to Rome. Everyone knew if he went to Jerusalem, he would be arrested by the Jewish religious leaders, but he seemed okay with that. Paul gathered many of his faithful followers and said good-bye, stating that his life meant nothing to him; all he wanted to do was finish this race and complete the job Jesus had given him—to tell everyone the good news! Paul knew he would not see any of these people again.

After his farewell speech, many cried and prayed for him. Paul sailed away toward Jerusalem. Along the way, they stopped at many ports. Many of Paul's disciples met him and tried to stop him from going to Jerusalem, knowing he would be arrested and handed over to the Romans. Paul only said, "The Lord's will be done."

Paul Under Arrest (ACTS 21-26)

Many people greeted Paul and his friends warmly when they arrived in Jerusalem, including James. They heard about all the people—Jews and non-Jews—who received Jesus.

That joy turned to chaos when Paul's enemies saw him in town and stirred up the crowds against him. They grabbed Paul, beat him, and were ready to kill him with stones when a Roman army stepped in and saved him. The Romans wrapped him in chains and took him to the prison until they could figure out what was going on.

Paul asked to speak to the crowd. He gave them his background as a nonbeliever who attacked the church,

then told about his amazing meeting with Jesus on that road to Damascus that changed his life. He said the Lord gave him a mission to the Gentiles.

The crowd went crazy and wanted him to die. The Roman commander ordered Paul to be whipped, but they backed off because Paul told the centurion he was a Roman citizen, and Roman citizens weren't treated this way.

They took Paul to the Sanhedrin, made up of Sadducees, Pharisees, and the high priest. Paul was clever. He knew the Sadducees didn't believe in a resurrection, so he told them about the resurrection, causing a huge argument to break out. It got so violent that the Romans took Paul away to safety. The Lord appeared to Paul that night and encouraged him to go to Rome.

A plot to kill Paul was revealed by Paul's nephew. Because Paul was a Roman citizen, the Roman commander ordered his soldiers to take Paul to Caesarea, the capital for the Roman government of Israel. They left at night with over four hundred soldiers guarding Paul. The governor, Felix, ordered Paul held for a trial. The high priest, Ananias; some elders; and a lawyer traveled to Caesarea and brought false charges against Paul.

Paul defended himself and told his story to Felix. Felix delayed a ruling and kept Paul in prison for over two years. Governor Festus took over for Felix and left Paul in prison.

The Jewish religious leaders presented more charges to Festus against Paul. Paul again defended himself. He then requested to speak to Caesar, the main leader of all of Rome. It was a right a Roman citizen had to present his case to Caesar. Festus agreed.

King Herod Agrippa (the last of the Herods to call himself king) arrived in Caesarea to see Festus. Agrippa had heard of Paul and wanted to meet him. Paul spoke to Agrippa with respect and told his testimony of being a Pharisee who had attacked the church, then met Jesus and was now preaching Jesus everywhere. Festus told Paul he was out of his mind. Paul tried to convince Agrippa and Festus to become Christians. They refused, but they found no reason to bring charges against Paul. If Paul hadn't requested a trial before Caesar, they would have let him go. But that wasn't God's plan.

Paul's Fourth—and Last—Mission Trip (ACTS 27-28)

Paul set sail for Italy to stand trial before Caesar. They boarded a ship with other prisoners and stopped at a number of ports along the way. Julius, the Roman centurion in charge of getting them all there, liked Paul and let him get provisions from his friends for the voyage to Rome.

The winds made it difficult for ships to sail across the Mediterranean Sea. Paul, an experienced traveler, tried to tell the centurion to be careful or they would lose the ship and cargo. The centurion didn't listen to him.

As they sailed along the island of Crete, off the coast of Greece, a hurricane-force storm hit them. They could not secure the boat with an anchor and began throwing cargo overboard.

An angel visited Paul and told him to have faith; he would stand trial before Caesar. The angel told them to run the ship into the ground so everyone could be saved. Fourteen nights later, the crew ran the ship into the coastline. All 276 people on board were safe. Usually the guards killed the prisoners when there was a shipwreck, but the centurion was grateful for Paul's leadership and spared everyone's life.

They swam to the shore of an island they found out was called Malta. The islanders greeted them kindly and built a fire for all those who survived the shipwreck.

Paul was gathering wood for the fire when a snake jumped out and bit him. The islanders saw the snake hanging from Paul's hand. They believed their gods had judged Paul for a crime by allowing this to happen, but when Paul showed no side effects, they changed their minds and thought he was a god!

The chief official of the island, Publius, also welcomed them. His father was very sick in bed with a fever. Paul prayed for him and the man was healed. The islanders brought their own sick family members out, and they too were all cured.

Three months later, they prepared a ship and sailed to Rome. In Rome, Paul lived under arrest in a house with a soldier watching around the clock.

Paul asked the local Jewish leaders to meet with him. He told them his amazing story of meeting Jesus and the four journeys he made to tell others the good news.

Large numbers of people showed up at Paul's house, and he explained to them about the kingdom of God, the law of Moses, and the prophets, all to convince them that Jesus was the God and the Messiah they had all waited to see. Some believed, but others did not.

For two years, Paul stayed in that rented house and welcomed everyone who came to see him. He proclaimed the good news and taught about Jesus with boldness.

WHAT'S THE POINT?

▸ While the killing of Stephen was a bad thing, it did spark the spreading of the gospel all over the world. The Christians got comfortable where they lived, so God pushed them out to Asia, Africa, and Europe.

▸ Jesus correctly told them at the beginning of Acts that they would be his witnesses to Jerusalem, Judea, and Samaria, and to the ends of the world. Acts covers the spread of Christianity to all those places.

▸ Paul would do anything to tell people about Jesus. He risked his life over and over to tell others about his experience. What are you willing to do?

Final Word

The book of Acts ended without saying if Paul ever saw Caesar, the powerful leader of Rome. Since an angel told Paul twice that he would stand before Caesar, we assume he did. There's also no indication that the Roman leader at the time, Nero, ever gave his life to Jesus. In fact, Nero was a really bad guy, but God obviously wanted to give him a chance to hear about Jesus.

Though Paul lived many of his final years in chains, nobody could put chains on the gospel. Paul wrote many letters to churches and pastors to encourage them, such as:

- Romans
- 1 and 2 Corinthians
- Galatians
- Ephesians
- Philippians
- Colossians

- 1 and 2 Thessalonians
- 1 and 2 Timothy
- Titus
- Philemon

Other writers also wrote letters that were circulated around the churches, such as:

- Hebrews (not sure who the author was)
- James (Jesus' half brother)
- 1 and 2 Peter (Peter the apostle)
- 1, 2, 3 John (John the apostle)
- Jude (called himself the brother of James)

The last book of the Bible, Revelation, was written by the apostle John while he was in prison on an island called Patmos. God showed him a number of visions and clues about the end of the world. The purpose of the book was to show that God has all of history—past, present, future—in his hands and, in the end, God wins the battle over evil.

Jesus promised he would return to the earth someday soon, and he would gather all believers to be with him in heaven.

Everyone who believes in Jesus and gives their life to him will be resurrected from the dead, like Jesus, to live in a beautiful eternal home with God the Father and Jesus present right before their eyes.

Will that be you?